# PROCESSED FOR PURPOSE

## DANYELLE SCROGGINS

Unless otherwise indicated, Scriptures verses are from the taken King James Version of the Bible.

"Scripture quotations are taken from the New American Standard Bible®, Copyright © 1960, 1962, 1963, 1968, 1971, 1972, 1973, 1975, 1977, 1995 by The Lockman Foundation

Used by permission." (www.Lockman.org)

Published by:

Divinely Sown Publishing

**PROCESSED FOR PURPOSE**

Copyright © 2014; © 2024 Unless otherwise indicated, Scriptures verses are from the taken King James Version of the Bible.

All Rights Reserved. Printed in the United States of America. No part of this book may be used or reproduced in any manner whatsoever without written permission except in the case of brief quotations embodied in critical articles and reviews.

Special discounts are available for quantity purchases. For details contact the publisher at the address above.

Library of Congress Catalogue Number:

ISBN-13: 9780996003865

First Edition paperback Aug 2016; Second July 2024

Printed in the United States of America.

Cover Designed by Danyelle Scroggins

*I dedicate this book to my incredible husband and best friend, Reynard C. Scroggins Sr., and my loving mother, Helen Quaker Hall. Your unwavering support and love has shaped me into who I am today. Because of your journeys and our shared process, I have come to understand the profound meaning of 'Faith to Faith' and I will always cherish and love you both.*

# ABOUT PROCESSED FOR PURPOSE

**Processed for Purpose**, is a transformative guide that aims to help readers replace fear with faith during life's toughest moments. I have crafted this book to inspire readers to see their challenges as processes that lead to their true purpose.

**Processed for Purpose** challenges readers to reframe their problems, viewing them as essential steps in God's divine plan. This book is filled with practical advice, personal anecdotes, and spiritual insights that encourage readers to reflect on their past experiences and recognize how these challenges have shaped their journey.

Throughout the book, I emphasize that:

1. Nothing in life happens by chance.
2. Every experience has a purpose.
3. Effective prayer and faith is crucial during difficult times.
4. Problems should be viewed as processes leading to growth.

5. God often uses life's challenges to prepare us for His purpose.

By the end of the book, readers will be able to identify how their hardships have turned into blessings, understand the purpose behind their trials, and develop a stronger faith in God's plan.

*1 Peter 5:5-7 (NASB)*

*Likewise you younger people, submit yourselves to your elders. Yes, all of you be submissive to one another, and be clothed with humility for God resists the proud, But gives grace to the humble. Therefore humble yourselves under the mighty hand of God, that He may exalt you at the proper time, casting all your care upon Him, for He cares for you.*

## CHAPTER 1
## GOD IS IN THE PROGRAM

Blessings come, even in adversity. It's easy to feel blessed when everything falls into place effortlessly. It becomes a different story when the storm clouds gather and life throws curveballs your way. We often overlook the fact that even in those challenging moments, we are still fortunate.

I often think of a time when everything fell apart. My job was stressful, relationships were strained, and my health was taking a hit. It felt like the universe was conspiring.

Amidst the chaos emerged small moments of grace. A smile from a stranger, a supportive message from a friend, and the warmth of my family reminded me that blessings often come in unexpected forms. The little sparks of joy I saw were not random. They were small kisses from God to encourage me to keep going.

I realized blessings encompass more than just the good times, but also involve discovering strength and resilience in adversity. It's about recognizing that every challenge is an opportunity for growth and transformation. The moment I embraced this mindset, everything changed. Hope and faith colored my perspective on life.

I gradually saw the hidden blessings in every situation. The challenges faced at work motivated me to gain new skills and to venture into diverse career opportunities. Strained relationships taught me the importance of communication and empathy. The health challenges forced me to take better care of myself and prioritize my well-being.

Honestly, this journey was hard and time-consuming. There were days when I doubted myself and my newfound perspective. Each time, I told myself that growth is a process, and every small step forward is a win.

While continuing to navigate life's difficulties, I found solace in my faith. I believed everything had a reason, a divine plan, even if I couldn't see it then. This belief became my anchor, keeping me grounded during the storms and helping me stay afloat when the waves of life threatened to overwhelm me.

In retrospect, I realize that those challenging times presented some of the most profound blessings in my life. They taught me resilience, patience, and the power of a positive mindset. They taught me that blessings lie in imperfections and beauty in brokenness.

By embracing this truth, I discovered a newfound sense of peace and contentment. I've discovered that blessings are everywhere, even in unexpected places. With this new understanding, I felt prepared to confront any challenges that life presented, fully aware of the blessings that surrounded me.

In addition, I realized that when God is for you, He surpasses the world against you. Consider this perspective: starting a church service without knowing the directions or flow is unheard of. God never creates life on earth without knowing its direction. He's not some fly by the seats type of God.

His strategic approach allows Him to excel.

He understands what is effective for you.

He knows when you will stop and acknowledge Him for directives.

He knows that inviting Him in will bring out the best of you.

He knows he is the MVPD...Most Valuable Program Director.

All we have to do is read the program, adapt and align ourselves to the changes, and readjust when it is necessary.

## LET'S PROCESS

*Have you been going through something that you just don't understand why you? (Explain)*

*Have you ever thought God must have more for you than what you presently see? (Explain)*

*Have you ever wanted to give up or just throw in the towel concerning a situation or your present situation? (Explain)*

*If you answered yes to any one of these questions, this book is really for you. Keep reading and after the end of every chapter, write down what resonated in your spirit!! Happy Reading...*

## CHAPTER 2
## THE TURNING POINT

I have a little secret: anytime something happens suddenly in my life, I always know God is somewhere in the program, and He's up to something. Remember, in Acts when a mighty rushing wind came suddenly (Acts 2:2)? I believe God uses the winds of circumstance to change the trajectory of our lives suddenly. When we are humble, we look at things differently, and when life changes suddenly, we can withstand it, knowing our trust is in God. Well, it took a while for me to get it.

It took a while for me to really embrace that all things truly work for my good. It also took some time for me to see why my first response to trouble was to blame God. If the devil could keep me blaming God, he could block me from the blessings God has for me.

Sometimes, we want to throw the blame on anyone and everyone except ourselves. It's easier to cope with sudden changes if we have someone else to pin the fault on. Rarely do we ask what did I do to contribute to this turn of events? However, I've found that God brings about turning points that cause us to put everything into perspective.

For me, things came into perspective when I remembered the story from Acts, where the Holy Spirit descended upon the disciples like a mighty rushing wind. Just as the wind had transformed their lives in an instant, I believed that this unexpected twist in my journey held the potential for profound transformation.

When life changes suddenly, it's easy to become overwhelmed and lose sight of our faith. But when we approach these moments with humility, we open ourselves to the possibility of growth and transformation. We learn to trust in God and to see beyond the immediate challenges.

This turning point marked the beginning of a new chapter in my life. It taught me that sudden changes, while often unsettling, carry within them the seeds of new beginnings. It reinforced my belief that God is always at work, even during chaos, orchestrating events in ways we cannot comprehend.

I also came to grips with the truth that God never lies. That was big for me! See, if the devil can make you feel you are all alone, he can make God look like a liar. How? God has said to us He will never leave or forsake us. The first thing the devil tries is to convince us we are out here all by ourselves; that God has forsaken us. He force feeds us every thought scenario to tempt us to believe what we see, verses what we know. Even the thought of God not being there contradicts what God said.

Another turning point in my life unveiled when I understood fully that God will never leave me because He cannot lie. Say this, "God can't lie." Sometimes we have to silence the devil by openly speaking into our atmosphere what God has said. In these moments, not only does God produce a level of faith in us, but we also produce a deeper level of faith in God.

As I embraced this newfound perspective, I felt a sense of liberation. I no longer viewed sudden changes as threats, but as opportunities for divine intervention. I learned to trust the process, to lean into my faith, and to remain open to the unexpected blessings that life offered.

LET'S PROCESS

What does the author believe about sudden changes in life?

How did the story from Acts influence the author's perspective on unexpected events?

Why does the author emphasize the importance of not blaming God during difficult times?

How does the author suggest we should respond to the devil's attempts to make us feel alone?

What lesson did the author learn about God's truth and faithfulness?

Have you experienced a sudden change in your life that made you question your faith? How did you cope with it?

LET'S PROCESS

How can you apply the author's advice on approaching sudden changes with humility and trust in God?

What strategies can you use to remind yourself of God's promises during challenging times?

How can you support others who are struggling with unexpected changes and help them see the potential for growth?

## CHAPTER 3
## MY MARRIAGE BEGINNINGS

When I met my husband, he was a hardworking man who had been at the same job for over nineteen years. He earned a good salary and took excellent care of his family. My attraction to him wasn't based on his job or his ability to make money, but on his humility. I couldn't quite fathom how a man could be so humble, to where nothing seemed to bother him. In church, you often encounter your fair share of things that should or could bother you, but not my husband.

I would say, "Scroggins, you just let people walk all over you." His reply would always be, "You cannot walk over me and not run into my God. If you walk over me, you must petition my God and receive permission from Him." His confidence in God's protection from harm surpassed my mental capacity. My feeble mind thought, if you do me in, I'm going to do you in, which made life stressful. Wow! How I envied my husband. I realized I wanted the assurance and humility Scroggins had.

There were times I tried to fake it, pretending that things didn't bother me, but my pride always got in the way. I never wanted folks to feel like they were playing me. Yet, Scroggins, in his different way, seemed to come out on top even when people thought they were doing him in. I wanted what he had, but I had to learn that being humble or gaining humility is a process. No one just wakes up and decides, "Today, I am going to be humble." I wished it were that easy because if it had been, I would have just tried to fake it until I made it. But as Isaiah 29:13 reminds us, anything fake can never become real just because it looks or acts the same.

Achieving genuine humility requires God's help. God is all-knowing and as strategic as He is intentional. He knows when we genuinely desire humility and when we are ready to stop struggling with who we are and become who He has ordained us to be. Therefore, God uses what I call processes to help us gain humility.

I didn't consider my husband the apple of my eye because he was so good. He is gifted. Gifted people stand out, even in their way of thinking. Those of us who have gifts in other areas can understand this. Gifted individuals have a different thought pattern, and most of them who recognize that their gifts come from God are truly humble. I am neither blind nor stupid; I have run into many gifted folks who are proud.

Many gifted Christians are full of pride. Those who are commanded to live a life of humility struggle with humanity because they allow themselves to be consumed by the epidemic called "Me". They prioritize themselves, live for themselves, and as a result, self-righteousness and self-centeredness (my word) prevail.

When a man believes he operates in his gifting because it is naturally him or believes he owns it, he sometimes makes himself a gift. If you find a man full of pride, you will see a man who made himself a gift and never separated himself from his gifting. He took the gift from God as an attribute or characteristic of simply being him. They need to remember the gift is from God, and their character helps them to embrace the gift and operate accordingly. As 1 Peter 4:10 says, "As each one has received a special gift, employ it in serving one another as good stewards of the manifold grace of God."

By observing my husband, I learned that true humility is rooted in the understanding that everything we have is a gift from God. Scroggins' unwavering faith and humility became my guiding light, showing me that humility is not about thinking less of yourself but about thinking of yourself less. It's about recognizing that God gives us our gifts and strengths not for our glory but for His purpose.

This realization marked the beginning of my journey towards humility. I knew it wouldn't be easy, and it certainly wouldn't happen overnight. But with God's guidance and the example set by my husband, I embarked on this path with a heart willing to learn and grow. I learned to let go of my pride, to stop pretending, and to live authentically in the grace and humility that God had always intended for me.

As I embraced this journey, I found a sense of peace and

contentment that I had never known before. I realized that true strength lies not in asserting oneself but in surrendering to God's will and trusting His plan. And in this newfound humility, I discovered a deeper, more meaningful connection with God and with those around me.

ANY NOTE BEFORE YOU PROCESS

LET'S PROCESS

How do you respond to challenges or situations that test your humility?

Do you find yourself leaning on your own understanding, or do you seek God's guidance and strength to navigate these moments?

In what ways can you practice humility in your daily life, especially in situations where pride tends to take over?

Think of a time when someone else's humility had a positive impact on you. What did you learn from that experience?

How do you differentiate between true humility and simply hiding your true feelings to avoid conflict?

LET'S PROCESS

What steps can you take to ensure that you remain humble and grounded, even when you achieve success or recognition for your gifts?

# CHAPTER 4
# A GLIMPSE OF THE WORD

*"And whoever exalts himself will be humbled, and he who humbles himself will be exalted." (Matthew 23:12)*

God blesses us with gifts not so that we can exalt ourselves. Neither for us to appear good to the world, which hates us. Instead, He gives us gifts to assist one another in the kingdom. We receive gifts from God to showcase His grace through our lives, which in turn brings glory to Him.

When I first began preaching, it was difficult for a woman to go up into a church's pulpit because some brethren did not agree with women preaching the Gospel. The late Pastor Authur Washington, whom I loved for his humility, said to me, "Daughter, look at Luke 14 with me. Jesus teaches on the lowly place, so whenever you go into a sanctuary, never go to their pulpit. It's better for them to ask you up than to ask you down." I was angry. Because of the way they treated me, I concluded that so-called godly men would rather have me be a whoremonger than a preacher. As long as I had whoredom in my veins, preachers stayed in my face. But as soon as I turned from my wicked ways, they despised my gift of exhortation. I thank God for the late Pastor Washington because this lesson was part of my process.

That is why it is hard to find me in the good girl preacher cliques. I do not need a clique or connections to validate my calling or my gifts. All I need is the gift God has given me. I also need enough character to operate inside of my gifting and outside of myself. I need humility to walk in the calling and operate my gifting God's way. Like Andrew Wilson, I believe that there are no New Testament prohibitions on women preaching the gospel. I found out when I was about twelve years old that God gifted me, and I had no choice whether I'd use the gift because my gifting alludes to purpose. Where there is purpose, you become a target—not just for people, but for the enemy and the enemy within.

That may have startled you, but sometimes gifted people lean on the gift instead of the giver, becoming complacent and arrogant in everything they do. Humility makes you strive to bless the gift giver. I'm not concerned about whether a man accepts me. My concern is that I don't get lazy because of my gifting. That I never neglect studying to show myself approved. I can never treat the giver of the gifting like a pimp. Understanding that He (The Giver) could have chosen anyone else to give my gift to, makes me work hard to stay close to The Giver. He and I together are more than the world against me.

This is where many women miss the mark. They think that creating a coalition with one another will lead to acceptance. But you have to know, when God calls you, He validates you, and your gifting equips you. His acceptance of you is more than enough, and if you humble yourself, He will cause you to intertwine with kings and queens. I remember when I first got engagements. Sometimes I would pray to attend, and upon doing so, I would give a heartfelt sermon. However, they would then disappointingly inform me that they wouldn't compensate me, but instead give me a basket of trinkets to add to my kitchen drawer collection. Yes, I felt a certain type of way until God reminded me: you are my vessel, chosen by me, to do the work I have begun. Even if they never offer a single cent, remain humble and graciously accept whatever they choose to give as the blessing they seek.

LET'S PROCESS

How can you ensure that your gifts are used for God's glory and not for self-promotion?

What role does humility play in your spiritual journey and in the use of your gifts?

How do you handle situations where your gifts are not acknowledged or rewarded as you expect?

In what ways can you support and uplift others who are also using their gifts for God's kingdom?

How can you stay connected to the giver of your gifts and avoid becoming complacent or arrogant?

# NOTES

# CHAPTER 5
# THE PROCESS TO HUMILITY

Humbling is a process, and this process is not always pretty, but it's promising. Sometimes it starts by trusting God to get you to an engagement and back home. Now, let us deal with "the Process."

When I think about a process, one thing that always comes to mind is a pregnancy. One of the best feelings in the world is the coming together of two people who are married and in love for the sake of knowing one another. The Bible says concerning Adam, "And he knew his wife."

I need to say this: it is also a good feeling for those who are not married, but the guilt and ties that exist can drive you insane. Therefore, you had better be careful when you share yourself with men or women whom God has not joined you with. Before I move on, I want to tell you, woman or man: when you have sex outside of marriage, you sin against yourself, and all sin leads to death. Stop killing yourself!

To become impregnated, you typically have to go through

the process of having sexual relations. There are now other methods, but they too require certain procedures accomplished through processes. I hear the Lord saying right here, "Don't worry because it has not happened yet, Sarah. I'm waiting for you to praise me for your process, and when you understand I give life, I'm going to open your womb, Sarah. It shall be accounted unto you because of your faith."

Whoever that was for, I pray you receive the prophetic and understand that sometimes we have to wait, but in waiting, we must continue to believe. This is not just for a baby, but for anyone who has been praying and waiting for the birthing of a vision or a dream. Don't laugh at God, because He sees. If He said it, it shall be so, and so shall it be.

During the pregnancy, your body transitions. The same applies to the birthing of humility, but where they differ is that the birthing of the baby is up to God, while the birthing of humility is up to you. Although the beginning of the process was fantastic, the transitioning phases can make you wish you had never begun the process (like swollen feet, backaches, morning sickness, a swollen nose, etc.). It eventually gets better, but before it gets better, it gets worse. Labor pains are enough to drive you insane and make you swear to never get pregnant again. Like most women, you forget the process and sometimes, less than a year or three years later, you go back through the same process all over again.

When you look at the gift, the result of the nine-month process, you can appreciate the process for what it was worth. You may repeat the process, but you are now smarter and can try to make the process easier this time around. It may seem like I'm rambling, but if you stay the course, you will get exactly what I'm trying to lead you toward.

Just because you make the process easier does not mean it will be, but you can rest easy knowing the outcome will be greater than the going through. Another thing is, no matter what, this process is only nine months. I have seen no one pregnant for over nine months. The last thing is that no matter what date the doctor gives, no matter how phenomenal new technology is or how brilliant those ultrasounds look, the baby will only come when God says it's time. Even with being rushed into an emergency C-section, keep in mind that God is in control.

The same thing applies to the birthing of humility. While the birthing of the baby is up to God, the birthing of humility is up to you. God will orchestrate the processes by which you gain humility, but the length and duration of the process are entirely up to you. What may take me nine days to get may take you nine years, or vice versa. That is why it is important for you not to be fooled by the process.

Those fooled by the process think they can control it, trick it, walk away from it, avoid going through it, or ignore it. The process tricks you into believing it's yours, but I need to inform you that you may handle the process, but it does not belong to you and you cannot control it.

Humbling oneself is necessary to become exalted or experience spiritual growth. It is the method by which God has ordained and allowed; the procedure that walks you into purpose, exaltation, and spiritual growth. Having gifts does not automatically mean you have spiritually grown. Never think you have all the humility you need, nor that you can live without humility. Humbling yourself is necessary if you ever want to move from where you are in life now. To gain humility, you must go through and endure the process. Reggie McNeal states in his book *Practicing Greatness* that humility derives from the leader's awareness of where their source of strength lies. This awareness should never cause you to feel elevated above the ONE who even caused you to embrace your strength.

I get tons of calls, especially after speaking engagements, from young women wanting to sit at my feet or for me to mentor them. I do not have a problem with either; in fact, I am humbled by the fact God has used me in the processing period of someone else. Their hearts reveal they are not looking for strength through the connection, but trying to ease the process. Most of them are tired of being overlooked and not appreciated and feel that if they connect, they can come up because of the connection.

I am not throwing shade because I was there. I thought, Lord, if you just let me connect with Juanita Bynum, I would get my ministry up and going. The Lord had to remind me she had to go through the process, just like me. He could connect us and I would still be just Danyelle. Stop trying to avoid the process. Being overlooked and unappreciated are just emotions the enemy uses to kick you off track. Go through the process and grasp humility.

Every time I ran into Mother Eunice Johnson, I would become an armor bearer. I carried her purse, Bible, bags, keys, whatever she had, to serve her. Whether I saw her at church or at work, I took it upon myself to serve the Woman of God. Instead of trying to steal a spot at the top, I took the road at the bottom, and there is power in the process when you operate in humility. McNeal states that people often perceive service solely in terms of acts, which is too limiting, but servant leadership is an attitude, and service is an intended result, not just a specific action carried out for others.

To this day, I will still carry her purse, Bible, and whatever else she has, even though people call me pastor. My heart knows that what I do for others will encourage those I lead to live a life of humility.

I'm still taking the low road. Why? I found out that humble is the way. To every success I want to achieve, if I work, endure processing, and remain humble, I cannot be stopped. If you want to achieve eternal life and walk in your purpose, you must continually subject yourself to processing. People who are often fooled by the process walk around with the "woe is me" syndrome. They walk around depressed and stressed because of the circumstances coming up in their lives. Preachers all over the world have to counsel like crazy because parishioners are allowing the process to paralyze them; even some pastors.

Instead of seeing their circumstances as the process by which God is elevating them, they allow the enemy to speak destruction into their lives. They falter because of a process that was never meant to destroy, break, or kill them but created to produce in them a clean heart. Humility has a cleanliness attached to it. Humility cleanses your heart. I have never met a humble man who has not had to go through some things.

I even think about marriages. No one goes into a marriage disclosing all of their deep secrets of sin, but as you are together, the years bring about processes. These processes humble you and make the dynamics of oneness greater, but only if you do not allow the processes to break the marriage apart. If you allow the processes in marriage to humble you, you can experience long, happy years together. (Someone married needed this.)

I have never met a humble person who declared they mastered all of their processes on the first go around. Some things happened in my life repeatedly, and it was not until I mastered the process and learned what God needed me to know that I moved on to bigger processes. Notice I did not say, "I moved on to a problem-free life." I said, "I moved on to bigger processes."

God elevates those who love Him more than they think or thought He could. He honors them with gifts because He can trust them. When God has plans for you, He will process you until His plans become a part of your plans. When God purposes you, you go through a process, and you must remember this throughout the duration of this book.

LET'S PROCESS

*Name a time in your life when you know you walked in pride?*

*What did God allow to happen in your life to humble you?*

*Did the process of humility make you clean?*

*Will you determine this day that the process will not kill you?*

How do you respond to challenges or situations that test your humility?

Do you find yourself leaning on your own understanding, or do you seek God's guidance and strength to navigate these moments?

In what ways can you practice humility in your daily life, especially in situations where pride tends to take over?

LET'S PROCESS

Think of a time when someone else's humility had a positive impact on you. What did you learn from that experience?

How do you differentiate between true humility and simply hiding?

# NOTES

## CHAPTER 6
## ALL IN HOW YOU HANDLE IT

The processes you face to gain humility and enhance yourself as part of humanity are not always pretty or easy. Sometimes these processes can be challenging and hard. You might question, how can God allow His child to go through so many hard things in life but still expect them to love and live according to His will? Keep reading...

God never intends for the process to break you. When the process breaks you, it brings you to the awareness that you need more faith, love, humility, patience, forgiveness, etc.; more than you thought you were. It is easy for us to become believers and think our belief is all we need to live an abundant life. Your belief system alone does not increase your faith or work ethic, nor does it enhance your humility.

Your beliefs make it easy for you to desire to incorporate the attributes that make believing or living the life of a believer easier. It takes humility to obey God, and because I believe in God, I desire humility that will aid me in obeying His Word above my flesh. My spirit longs for a space to hear God's voice. This only happens when I'm humble enough to know there is a power above all powers and that all things that happen to me work for my good; to create a humbled me who recognizes God is, God does, and God knows.

The "it" in your life can cause disruption but will not cause destruction. I would love for everything around me to operate as I desire without disrupting my natural flow, but we do not live in a perfect world. When processes arise in my life, it is all in how I handle them that determines whether they will just disturb me or destroy me.

Remember, I told you my husband was a hardworking man. After 29 years of working, he got ill. Just before Reynard got sick, God allowed my husband and me to dream the same dream. I woke up and said, "Scroggins, you will never imagine what I dreamt." He said, "I hope your teeth didn't fall out." I said, "Yes!" He said, "Mine too."

Immediately, I asked God to show me what He was trying to relay to us. God gave me Psalm 30:5: "For His anger is but for a moment, His favor is for life; Weeping may endure for a night, but joy comes in the morning."

Scroggins and I had been living the high life. We were making good money, had a home in the city on an acre of land. We were driving a Lexus, Cadillac, and Expedition, and my daughter had her own car. Two of our children were in private school, were paying child support for his children, running a prosperous church, paying bills, giving away money, and living what we thought was life. Then God gave us this. We immediately started repenting, but did not know for what we were repenting. Have you ever reached a point of repentance when you thought you were perfectly right? I learned through this that I am filth even in my best state, and my act of repentance is a daily must-do!

We both came into agreement that God was angry with us, and although He was angry, that did not stop His favor. Our hearts accepted that weeping would arise and eventually joy would find us. We did not know it then, but God was getting ready to allow us to go through a process that would change our lives forever.

We could have pleaded with God to allow whatever we were about to face to pass over us, but we were both tired. We were tired of playing God in the lives of the people, giving folk money whenever they called, living a lie—pretending to be happy but dying on the inside—and tired of living with means that made enemies friends and friends enemies. I have a dear brother in the Lord, Bishop Jones (who is the Leader of Eden Worship Center in Shreveport, Louisiana), who says, "It's the Savior complex." This is when you take on God's job because you are able, and the people expect you to fix their situations and not God (Pastor J. Gregory Jones). Wow!

Barely two months later, God revealed the "it." Scroggins walked out of his job, and the mortgage company I was working for faltered. Here we were with a $1300.00 house note, two car notes, and the only money coming in was his dad's SSI. We could no longer afford the building for the church, so we gave up the house and moved to another house big enough to accommodate the church. One by one, every car we had got wrecked. All this happened in less than a year. I got a job at a loan place because we still had two in private school and one in college. He was now getting behind on his child support, and with the little job I had and his dad's money, we could not afford to pay it.

We moved into my best friend's rental home, and in a little more than a year, God took his dad home and a few months after told me to leave that job. If I had never questioned God before, I did big time. I could not imagine how He was going to allow all of this to happen to us. Then, on top of all that, He kept showing me how the job I had did not fit into His will for my life. I felt so convicted every time I processed a loan, but it took the opposition of them not letting me off to go to one of my children's games for me to leave.

God told me years ago I was a mother, and mothers supported their children. My job or nothing else would ever keep me from doing what I needed to do for my children, and God knew this. I was hanging on to my job for dear life, and God knew the only way I would ever walk away was to make them tell me I couldn't leave to go support my child. You talk about a rock and a hard place, but when you are a young mother growing with the children who saved your life, you will let nothing stop or hinder you from being there for them.

My aunt gave us a car, and a few months afterward, we had a bad rainstorm, and the car got flooded out. As I am writing this now, I'm seriously laughing, but you can believe it was not a funny matter when we were going through it. Things were so crazy that Scroggins and I would look at one another and laugh. Then the house we were living in got sold, and we had to move again. Mind you, we had his parents' home in the country, but we did not have transportation to move back there. Scroggins, as sick as he was, went back to work, and I spent my days praying.

I kept saying to God, "I trust you, Lord," and crying, "Please forgive us." The only difference is now I knew what I was repenting for. I had been playing god in the lives of people. Call me for money, and I gave it. Ask me, and I supplied. Never did I ask God if this was who He wanted me to bless. God couldn't let people go through for me bailing them out. Then He showed me how He would shut them down concerning me.

We were now car-less and living in the home of my godchildren's aunt. We couldn't even get a ride to the grocery store, and when we asked one of our friends to pick Scroggins up for work, they told him to meet them at the corner four blocks away. I watched my husband hop up the street with the nerve problem in his hip, thinking, "Lord, if you forgive us, please allow our night to be over." Despite all our prayers, Scroggins and I decided we were going to continue to praise God through this process. Did I cry sometimes? Yes, I did. Did I pray? All the time. More importantly than all of that, I developed a praise that was real. I now call it my "anyhow praise." No matter what we were facing, I was going to praise God anyhow.

This is what I mean by "all in how you handle it." You can choose to allow the situation that surrounds your process to take you under, or you can praise your way through. We decided we loved God too much not to trust Him, and He loved us too much to allow the present circumstance to kill us. People always say, "What doesn't kill us only make us stronger." Some of them don't truly grasp the truth in what they are saying. The process should never overwhelm or break you. It uncovers your misuse of life and your lack of faith concerning God's promises. The uncovering of what you lack should lead to the well again.

That went over somebody's head. See, you will never live life to the fullest until you lay down your life. When you understand nothing just happens and you realize God will allow things to do one of these things: humble you, spur spiritual growth or maturity, reveal the real you (your heart), uncover your sins, or strengthen someone else. It leads you to God's fountain, with a prayer directed to gain that which you lack. Embrace this and you will be more apt to handle your going through as if "YOU WIN" from beginning to the end.

## LET'S PROCESS

How do you respond to challenges or situations that test your humility?

Do you find yourself leaning on your own understanding, or do you seek God's guidance and strength to navigate these moments?

In what ways can you practice humility in your daily life, especially in situations where pride tends to take over?

Think of a time when someone else's humility had a positive impact on you. What did you learn from that experience?

How do you differentiate between true humility and simply hiding your true feelings to avoid conflict?

# DECLARATION

*I declare at this moment that I am victorious. I understand it appears to me and others that my surroundings and my circumstances don't equal victory, but I refuse to live my life based upon what things appear to be. As I look deeper, I see an all-knowing God at work in my life. He is leading me into victory and with my hands lifted up, I praise Him in advance. For nay in all things, be it rough, tough, bad, hurtful, painful, or just downright stressful, I am more than a conqueror.*

## CHAPTER 7
## VICTIM TO VICTOR

Even when I am going through the worst of times, I must always remember that I am not a victim, but a victor. I know someone is saying, "How in the world can I fake like I'm a victor when I could be on the top ten victims list right now?" Understand that no matter what happens to you, God is in full control. You must, despite your present state of awareness, know this:

"Yet in all these things we are more than conquerors through Him who loved us" (Romans 8:37).

Amid feeling like a victim, if I trust God at all, my spiritual hindsight kicks in and assures my intellectual capacities that no matter what it looks like, how I feel, or how bad I'm hurting right now, I'm still a conqueror. When it all boils over, I'm at the top. I'm not too prideful to take you through my journey of victimization so you can see that the same God who brought me out has the will and power to do the same for you.

Take a piece of roast, put it in a pot of boiling water, and as long as it stays in the pot long enough, it will be tender and good. Sometimes, God will put you in the pot, and although the hot water hurts, you will come out better than you went in. I also found that the more I add to the pot, like seasonings, onions, and bell peppers, the better the roast tastes. No, you are not a piece of meat, but sometimes it feels like you have to endure being plunged into boiling water. If you just keep adding pieces of the Word of God to your heart while you are being boiled, you will come out tasting, smelling, and looking like a conqueror. God anointed you to go through this—just praise Him during this situation.

I was speaking with one of my friends, and she said to me, "Scroggins, I just feel like the victim." I replied, "Well, tell the victim you already have the victory!" Call me crazy, unintellectual, or whatsoever you choose, but every now and again, I have to remind myself that I already have the victory and I am anointed for this right here." This is exactly why James says in James 1:2, "My brethren, count it all joy when you fall into various trials, knowing that the testing of your faith produces patience."

How on earth can I still be joyful while going through? I understand it's just another opportunity for me to prove to the world, myself, and my God that I know through this, He's going to produce a Danyelle that believes it's already alright and has the patience to wait on the manifestation of a victorious breakthrough!

Now get this: you may say, "How can I feel victorious when my body, my knees, my legs, my back, etc., are immersed in pain?" I understand because my knee hurts too.

Sometimes I go to bed and feel worse when I awake, but when my knee hurts the most, I think of my friend Linda who has no leg.

See, I am not victorious because I have two legs and she doesn't, but I am victorious because I have sense enough to know that if she can live victoriously with one leg, surely I can with two legs despite the pain! When we think about the goodness of Jesus and all that He has done for us, we ought to be more willing to make the declaration, "I am a victor, even when I feel like a victim."

I know someone may say that this is easy to do when things are going well, and somehow people think that pastors always have pleasant moments. I am here to tell you; they do not. Their struggle is just as real as yours, often more intense. The only difference between a real man or woman of God is that they truly believe all things will work for their good and none of the things they encounter break them. They instinctively know if God allowed this occurrence to flow their way —He's getting ready to do something greater in their lives. God is such a God who, when He has granted you a life of greater, will strengthen you for what lies ahead.

Could this very well be for a layperson as well? Of course. Look at 1 Peter 5:9-10:

"Resist him, steadfast in the faith, knowing that the same sufferings are experienced by your brotherhood in the world. But may the God of all grace, who called us to His eternal glory by Christ Jesus, after you have suffered a while, perfect, establish, strengthen, and settle you."

The enemy has sought to devour you and use the hardships some of you are facing right now to destroy you literally. Our greatest power comes when we resist him! When you absolutely refuse to allow the enemy to cause you to feel defeated and you believe God will, you can rest knowing that somewhere one of your fellow brethren has not only gone through what you are experiencing right now, but has overcome. Then the prayer takes effect: "May the God of all grace, who called us to His eternal glory by Christ Jesus, after you have suffered…"

See, not before you suffer or during the suffering, but afterward… I want to declare to you there really will be glory after this! Whatever your "this" is, after you have experienced discomfort, pain, tears, abuse, loneliness because of it, God is going to perfect, establish, strengthen, and settle you. See victory in perfection! Anticipate victory in the establishment! I see victory in strength! I see victory in the settlement!

Your faith becomes perfected because every time you believe God can and will do it, and He actually does, it elevates your faith to the next level. You perfect your walk because when you understand the value in your Christian walk and see the devil trying to shake you off course, you take off those stilettos and put on your Converse so you can endure in all kinds of weather. See, my pumps might make me a little shaky, but Converse makes me flat-footed. Now don't get me wrong, somebody might be more stable in their stilettos, and by all means, do whatever you do to make your walk secure! (Ha-ha)

Just know whatever God allows during your process cannot stand close to the promise you will receive after it is over. All you have to do is stay the course, don't lose heart, do not faint, and pray your way through. You know when you communicate with the Father—He has a way of making you feel at ease. Communication with the Father is necessary during your processing. Why? He is the only one who can direct you to the truth found in His Word when you are at the point of giving up and giving in. God's Word will encourage you!

I know you can be like David and encourage yourself, but baby, I'd rather God's encouragement over mine any day. There is nothing like going in prayer and just waiting for an answer from the Lord. I'm finding that because we all want those right-now fixes, prayer is sometimes the last option when it should have been your first move. We will discuss this later, but I would have you remember that as a victim, God has not given you a spirit of fear. People who are scared give in to whatever or whoever is victimizing them, but those with love, power, and a sound mind rely on God for guidance and persist in fighting until they achieve victory.

LET'S PROCESS

How do you maintain a victor's mindset during challenging times?

What practical steps can you take to remind yourself of God's control and promises when you feel overwhelmed?

Can you recall a time when you felt like a victim but later saw how the experience made you stronger?

How does your faith influence your ability to persevere through difficult processes?

In what ways can you support and uplift others who may feel like victims, helping them see their victory through Christ?

Name a time in your life when you know you walked in pride?

LET'S PROCESS

What did God allow to happen in your life to humble you?

Did the process of humility make you clean?

Will you determine this day that the process will not kill you?

# NOTES

## CHAPTER 8
## YOUR FAITH IS IMPERATIVE

Notice how I said in the chapter prior, "The only difference between a real man and woman of God is they truly believe all things will work for their good." I really want you to get this chapter if you get nothing else in this book. The real people of God understand Satan does not care about anything you have. We have grown so accustomed to blaming the devil for small junk he is allowing you to destroy your very own livelihood with your words. The one thing the devil desires more than anything you have is YOUR FAITH! All the destruction and circumstances that rock your world or cause you distress are just tokens to cause your FAITH to become non-existent.

The stark reality is without FAITH, you cannot even believe God exists. Therefore, I am rocked to my core when I hear folks who are going through say, "If there were a God, I wouldn't have to go through all of this."

Their circumstance has caused them to doubt the very existence of God. A person who is unsure won't ever gain stability in their belief because, as sure as you live on this earth, circumstances will be attached to your walk.

Hear me now... if I only rely on stability in my surroundings to keep my faith stable, then it is not true faith at all. It is contentment as long as things are good. Faith is only evident when things are bad, and the contentment is still there. That is why Paul said in Philippians 4:11-13:

"Not that I speak in respect of want: for I have learned, in whatsoever state I am, therewith to be content. I know both how to be abased, and I know how to abound, everywhere and in all things I am instructed both to be full and to be hungry, both to abound and to suffer need. I can do all things through Christ which strengtheneth me."

Paul is saying no matter the circumstance, because I have FAITH in God who framed the world by His Word, all I have to do is believe that if I have Him and His Word, I can do all things through Him, the ONE who can strengthen me. For those of you who are not Bible readers, I've jumped to Hebrews 11:6, which starts by saying, "But without faith it is impossible to please Him, for he who comes to God must BELIEVE (have FAITH) that He is and that He is a rewarder of those who diligently seek Him."

Real folks' faith keeps them in SEEK MODE because they understand that although it may not be good right now, they are seeking God who can bring them out and through. And because they're in SEEK MODE, God will eventually go into REWARD MODE! I keep throwing that word "real" out there. Why? There is a difference between religious folks and kingdom folks! Religious folks fake it until they make it, but Kingdom folks faith it until they make it.

When you become Kingdom-minded, you understand that FAITH is imperative; vitally important to your kingdom's walk and existence. If the Word of God framed the world, then the Creator has influenced everything that exists, although I may not see it. That is why Jesus says in Luke 10:19, "Behold, I give unto you power to tread on serpents and scorpions, and over all the power of the enemy: and nothing shall by any means hurt you." When you believe and have faith in One whose words have shaped your surroundings, then you please God!

Repeat this: I please God because my talk, my actions, and my life denote that I believe in God.

Now let me hit here. Can you see why the devil does not want your stuff and all he wants is your FAITH? When he can destroy the very core of your being, then he has done something. What are you talking about, Danyelle? See, out of all the things God gave me in this human body, the one thing that means the most is my measure of faith. Romans 12:3 says, "For I say, through the grace given unto me, to every man that is among you, not to think of himself more highly than he ought to think; but to think soberly, according as God hath dealt to every man the measure of faith."

See, my gifting is only operable because of the measure (me believing that God gave me what He gave me to operate in the body of Christ as a Kingdom participant), and my measure becomes increased only as my belief in the Word increases.

The more Word I get, the more faith I get, we assume. Not

necessarily so. Some folks get plenty of the Word... Wednesday night, Sunday morning, or every time you or I walk into God's house. The irony of getting the Word is knowing and recognizing what season you are in. Sometimes you're in the season of faith-building—this is when you embrace every Word heard, building upon the measure of faith you have; you embody the Word as though it's all you have to stand upon and you hunger for it and thirst after it. Other times, you're in faith-testing—this is when the Word is pricking at you to try it; you desire the Word as cheat points to the test; you hear it but only exercise it as a dare or as Russian roulette. Then there's faith fertility—this is when you get the Word, but in parts, like seeds; you hear all of it, but only parts of it penetrate through all the other fifty million thoughts rattling in your head. Finally, there's faith instability—when you just occupy space where the Word is heard, and although you've seen it work for others, your thinking is not stable enough to apply it to your own life.

Just know when you are being processed, if you do not have faith, you will never find out what your purpose is. The measure of faith is your mode of operations. Like a car's primary mode is the motor, so is your faith to your body or human life. If you lack faith, you will never uncover your purpose. Without faith, you will never achieve peace and cannot accomplish your earthly assignment. I had to believe I could preach the Gospel before I did it. Witnessing women preaching, I felt a strong conviction that said, "I can do that too."

Without me thinking that or allowing my measure to stir

up that gift, I would be someone rocking the days away, never to be known as one who preached the Gospel.

## LET'S PROCESS

What does the author say Satan desires more than anything else you have?

Why does the author believe blaming God during difficult times can be detrimental to one's faith?

What is the difference between faith and contentment, according to the author?

How do you react to sudden changes or challenges in your life? Do you find yourself blaming God or questioning your faith?

What strategies can you use to strengthen your faith during difficult times?

## LET'S PROCESS

How do you discern the 'season' of faith you are currently in? What steps can you take to move towards a season of faith-building?

What practical steps can you take to ensure your faith remains strong and unwavering, even when your surroundings are unstable?

How can you incorporate more of God's Word into your daily life to build and test your faith effectively?

What changes can you make in your life to transition from being a 'religious' person to a 'Kingdom-minded' person as described by the author?

# NOTES

## CHAPTER 9
## GOD IS STILL IN CHARGE

Processing people is difficult to understand because you see them in their current state, while they see themselves in the state they hope for. People who know who their God is can smile amid pain and adversity. They walk around as if nothing is wrong. As the saying goes, "They smile on the outside while crying on the inside." Let me tell you, not all tears are bad tears. Sometimes, I was crying on the inside saying to myself, "Oh, but when God gets through with me!" or "Just wait until they see the finished product."

You might wonder what happened with our house situation. The godchildren's aunt decided she wanted to come back home, and of course, this meant we had to go. We moved to my best friend's house, and it's hard to live in peace in someone else's place. Scroggins and I were talking, and it was apparent he was ready to go. I started going to the country every day to fix up his parents' home. It was as if I was going to work. I had a little maintenance worker who would sometimes be high as a kite, but he helped me, and I had faith that we would get this house ready to live in.

Before I knew it, we had the floors stable enough to walk on and the plumbing durable enough to work. When Scroggins came in, I said to him, "Baby, we are leaving as soon as God says go." There was no electricity because the mortgage company received a thousand-dollar check to pay the electric bill and paid nothing. I could have been angry, but I refused to give the devil the victory. We used the light of the day and jugs of water for baths. As I type now, the tears are flowing. Just remembering where we came from makes me acutely aware that God will fix it for you.

I was getting behind on the private school tuition and paying as I could. Months prior to the move home, Scroggins and I were at the Family Dollar. Scroggins went into the store, and a black man drove up beside our car. I looked over, and he beckoned for me to let the window down. When I did, he said, "You know what you are supposed to be doing, right?"

"No sir, what am I supposed to be doing?" I asked.

"God told you months ago to go back to school. If you go back to school, it's going to keep you from being homeless. The school funds are going to pay your bills, and your job will pay them back," he said.

I cried because God had told me to go to school. Then my aunt confirmed it by one day out of the blue, asking me what was stopping me from going to school. Then my oldest daughter said to me after I helped her with a paper and she received an A, "Mom, you could get A's if you went to school." Now, this was the fourth confirmation, and I understood. Every financial aid check I received, I paid tuition and kept gas in the car.

Mind you, we still had no electricity or water. I went to the library every day. Let me tell you, when you are determined to take up your bed and walk, you will do things you never thought you would do.

I got to the children's school, and the woman who took the payments berated me for being late. I got so angry, and God in heaven knows I felt like cussing her out and jumping across the desk at her. Just when the one word hit my thoughts, the Lord spoke firmly, "Go." With tears running down my face, I went to the counselor's office to withdraw my child. She did not know I was paying tuition instead of eating, going to bed some nights praying God would supply food. Her blatant disregard for what we might go through and my obedience to His right-now command caused God to open up the windows from heaven upon us.

God moved upon the heart of a special woman, and not only did we have electricity the next day, but we also had water. God will use a heart hardened towards you to be the reason someone blesses you. You had better hear God. When He says, "Don't," you had better stop. When He says, "Move," you had better move. Whatever God tells you to do, just do it!

People do not close or harden their own hearts towards you; God does it. He will cause the very person who is in earshot of your blessing to hate you with a passion. This hatred is to lead you into prayer for your enemies because when you pray for your enemy, the word you release in private prayer gets an open reward. Hallelujah, somebody! Stop trying to figure out why folks don't like you or why they act cold towards you and start thanking God for producing an enemy to elevate your prayer life and make your blessings visible.

You could not have told us years prior we would face what we were facing, but even in our place as it was, we were still collecting blankets to give to homeless people in the winter. God will cause you to bless others, even in your mess. Now, we didn't have the "Savior Complex," we had the "Giver's Attributes." We learned we had to sow ourselves out of the mess we were in.

I feel led to go here... I don't hold ill will towards the woman in the office because she made me declare I'd never be so low that another person feels they can talk and treat me any kind of way. Her inability to discern that I was a hurting woman lit a fire in me, and I thank God for her to this day.

I don't know where you are right now in your life, but just in case you are right where we were, I have two words that won't cost me anything to give and you nothing to receive... TRUST GOD! He is still in charge, and when He finds you fit for the process, He will bring provisions to encourage you to hang on to His promises. God trusts you enough to be processed like this; you should trust Him enough to know that if you just simply obey His Word, His will is going to prevail in your life.

I have not seen the man who pulled next to us at the store,

and I am convinced God sent an angelic presence to help me with a piece of the puzzle. I have a psychology degree, and every financial aid check kept us from being on the streets. My God, today! During this time, I opened up channels of finances by doing all kinds of work. I was building websites, printing flyers, typing letters, doing weddings, whatever I could do to bring in a dollar.

God started sending me business from everywhere. It seemed like every time we got down to our last dime, He'd send me some more work. Then the unthinkable happened. Scroggins, who was already sick but struggling to work, came home feeling horrible. I had a dream that night after he went to bed... we were going to miss one of Raiyawna's games because his daddy would not stay in the grave. I went to make him lie back down, and he refused. He clearly wanted Reynard. So, I called Reynard, and he came to the graveyard. Reynard told me to leave him, but he promised he'd come to the game and would not stay in the graveyard.

Little did I know, God was giving me assurance concerning what was about to happen. Two days later, Scroggins went to the hospital to get a shot. Normally, when they gave him a shot, he would get better, but this time, nothing helped. He was in the bed and had stopped eating. Then he got so weak, he could not walk to the bathroom. I had to put him on my back and drag him to the bathroom. I sat him on the toilet and ran across the street to tell his cousin I needed help to get him in the car. My husband was bleeding like crazy.

We made it to the LSU Health Science Center, and they

quickly took him to the back. Mother Eunice, who was a chaplain at the hospital, came to be with me, and she and I prayed. I rebuked the death angel, and not five minutes later, the patient, two doors down from Scroggins died. Scroggins was going into renal failure, but God! In a matter of two years, my poor husband was struggling in his body. So not only were our finances under the process umbrella, but his health was also as well.

All I could do was remind him he promised me he would not stay in the graveyard. I was not ready to be without my husband, and I knew God gave me the warning so I would not abort the process. God wanted me to remember that no matter what happened, He was still God, and He was still in control of our process. After three full weeks in the hospital, Scroggins came home feeling better but still battling.

I hear the Lord telling me to tell the dreamers, don't think it crazy that I have caused you to dream. Do not take the dreams as just a natural occurrence. God says, I give the dreamer dreams so that they may see what is to come and hold on through the process. I always give you a dream so that you will govern your flesh accordingly because it is your flesh that will cause you to abort the dream or consider it null, thus voiding out a piece of your life's puzzle. When you are being processed, you will experience some things you never thought would happen to you in a million years. Do not fret. The same God who allowed you to be processed will keep you while you are being processed. If the process fools you, you will stress, and stress has the power to take on many forms. I believe that the fooling of the process was weighing heavy on my husband BUT GOD!

Sometimes I had to encourage my husband and myself. That is why it's important for wives to be girded with the Word of Truth. Your husband needs more than a sex partner, another mother, or a money spender. He needs someone who will pray and go before the Throne of Grace when he is too weak to go for himself. He needs his helper!

LET'S PROCESS

Why do you think it is challenging to understand people in their current state versus their aspirational state?

How does faith influence the ability to endure pain and adversity with a positive outlook?

What was the significance of the encounter with the man at the Family Dollar?

What is the difference between having a "Savior Complex" and "Giver's Attributes" according to the author?

# NOTES

## CHAPTER 10
## TRUSTING GOD'S GPS

In all you are facing, God will direct you if you acknowledge Him. Proverbs 3:6 says, "In all thy ways acknowledge Him, and He shall direct your paths." Some of us use the GPS (Global Positioning System) instead of the real GPS (God's Positioning Services). God has the plan already mapped out, and if you take a little time to acknowledge Him concerning your moves, He will point you in the best direction. Some of us would rather journey on instinct, thinking it's best to go left, but instinct partnered with God-given instructions is instrumental and important. If you acknowledge Him, He will place you in the location where you will serve according to His will and bring glory to His name.

Get this: there's no point in acknowledging that you need the real GPS and then not following the directions. Not all of His directions will make sense to you. Sometimes He will give directions that seem out of touch with whom you are, and sometimes they seem unorthodox. Remember, His thoughts and ways are not like ours. You are not dealing with an ordinary individual;; you are dealing with a God who is unconventional, uncompromising, unwavering, faithful, just, intelligent, and all-knowing.

During this process, God would direct me to give or do something for someone that required no money. Imagine that—having no money already and being told to spend hours blessing someone just because He said to do it. This is the hardest lesson for givers. People who are givers just like to give; they never take the time to ask God if this is the cause they should be giving to. They just do it with no instructions or directions because it comes naturally to them. Givers, you will never bless God in your giving until you understand that He who created you as an instrument of giving is the ultimate guide. Your gift of giving will never surpass the one who designed you to be a giver.

Stop using your gift as a giver to get people to notice or celebrate you. You are an instrument of God's design to do as He pleases. You are God's hands in the earth realm, and when you understand how important you are, you will give Him full advantage of the use of your hands for His cause. If you would just get this: when He uses you as His earthly hands, He releases through you the benefits of His promises to the beneficiary that's worthy of the benefit at that moment. Sometimes, when you give against His directions, His benefits fall on cement ground and get crushed.

If you give my children my death benefits before I die, then you prematurely abort the honor due to me as their mother. They may treat me any kind of way, knowing that they have already received their inheritance. When they have to wait for the benefits, they believe that good morals and good works will cause them to get more. That is how it is with some folks and God. If they believed they would be blessed and could live any way they desired, they would do just that.

As a giver, you must not operate in the capacity of your gifts to satisfy yourself or man. You must remember you are God's hands, and His hands don't reward inappropriate behavior. When I understood this, I could hear Him say, "Bless her," "Do this for him," "Give her this," etc.

During this time, I had to speak at a church. Somebody somewhere is giving the Word and struggling like crazy. Preaching God's Word was sometimes the only way I could keep my mind from trying to fix the process in my favor. When I was preaching God's Word, everything was perfect, even my jacked-up, lacking life.

After the service, God told me to ask for the website of the woman who spoke the Word after me. We exchanged numbers, and I felt a sisterly connection towards her, which I rarely felt. I had gotten to where I and women in ministry didn't mix. It seemed when they weren't judging me for who I used to be; they were using me or trying to fit me into cliques. Feeling this way towards this young woman was shocking and strange. When I got home and went to her website, I heard God immediately say, "Fix it."

I worked day and night, and when I called her, I asked if I could help her. When she said, "Yes," I sent her to her new website. We cried and screamed together. I knew I was following the directions of the Most High, and she knew it was His doing! There is nothing like following God's directions and the excitement you feel when you know you did what He said.

After this experience, she and I became good friends, and we still keep in contact to this day. There was more direction concerning her. She received an assignment to speak at a church in DeSoto, Texas, and I posted the flyer on her page. Scroggins and I were up early one Saturday, and the Lord said for us to go. We only had enough gas money to get us to Texas and back home, but I knew I heard God. I picked up the phone and found out his family was giving his cousin (whom I call uncle) a birthday party, so we made a grand trip out of it —go to church and then to the party.

The service was phenomenal, and she was so excited we surprised her. Better than that, at the very end, the Pastor of the church was praying and prophesying into the lives of the people. I have always been told that prophecy leads you to God or towards His direction, brings a warning, or encourages the heart of the believer. I also know that if I'm not called out, that is okay. Rarely does anyone call me out, because God often tells me exactly what He needs me to know. On this day, I couldn't help but think how outstanding the atmosphere was and how anointed the man of God was.

Just when the pastor spoke into the last life and was heading to the pulpit, he heard God directing him. He turned around and said to Scroggins and me that God was getting ready to take us into a wealthy place. He said we were going to have to go through something, but after it was all over, God would get the glory. Then he screamed. Scroggins and I both fell under the anointing, and when we were alert enough to get up, he screamed again, and we went back down.

When we finally mustered enough strength to get up, there was such a heavy praise coming from us. I almost cannot even explain the praise. It was so different, so intense, yet so exhilarating. As we drove to the birthday party, we couldn't help but laugh. We laughed because we believed we had already experienced the worst of the worst. How could things possibly get any worse or more complicated than they already had? We did not know, but one thing we knew was that God directed us to DeSoto, Texas, to get another piece of the process. I am thankful we obeyed His directions. God can direct you, and all you have to do is follow the direction. Don't figure it out; follow it through.

## LET'S PROCESS

*Is God Your Guide?*

*How easy is it for you to follow the directions God has set before you?*

*Consider all the steps you've made in your life thus far, now take the time to write them out here...*

*Can you see God in the steps you've made even though you thought you were being creative?*

# NOTES

## CHAPTER 11
## A FAITHFUL WALK THROUGH FIRE

A few months later, I prepared for my annual Women's Conference, held on the first weekend of December. On December 5, 2012, Scroggins (my hubby), my good friend Jacqueline Antwine, and I had just finished a long day of running errands. We picked up conference t-shirts, visited Scroggins' sick cousin, grabbed last-minute items from the store, and bought some bologna. Jackie and I planned to go home and pack conference bags because the next day, Thursday, would mark the start of the Women at the Well Conference.

Last Wednesday, we were all together, but I decided Jackie and I would go to Bible Study with Scroggins. This Wednesday, I debated going, but knew I had too much to get done before Thursday night. While Jackie will help, I felt the need to finish. Scroggins affirmed we needed to stay home and get everything done.

Scroggins was waiting for our baby boy, Gabriel, who had

not followed the after-school instructions correctly. Gabriel had youth practice for an upcoming event and needed to accompany his father to New Vessels. When Gabriel finally arrived, despite his dad's reprimand, I quickly fixed him a bologna sandwich and laughed that he couldn't get anything but mustard because of his disobedience. I followed him to the door and said to Scroggins, "Be careful now." Then I closed the door, and Jackie and I instantly started working and munching on sandwiches.

Usually, Scroggins calls me when he makes it to the church, but he doesn't. I picked up my phone, dialed his number, and the call went straight to voicemail. I hung up but felt uneasy. When our routines break, it makes us uneasy because we live by routines. About ten minutes later, someone started pounding on my front door. I realized I was not even wearing pants. Jackie was sitting on the opposite end of the couch, and I had left my door unlocked. Whoever it was could have come in and done whatever to us.

I really wanted to jump up and lock the door but shakily asked, "Who is it?" The voice said, "Myesha." Even when she stated her name, I knew something was wrong. I immediately thought it was Scroggins' aunt, who was well into her nineties. As she opened the door at my request, all I can remember her saying was, "Reynard's been in a bad wreck, and he is being airlifted to the hospital." I said, "How do you know?" She told me her aunt had told her. Then I asked, "How does she know?" She said her sister told her. I asked, "Can you take me to him?" She said, "Let me go get my sister and my car keys."

Subsequently, I stood up, walked into my bedroom, and

instantly begun praying. I cannot tell you or anyone else exactly what I was thinking, but I knew God gave Scroggins to me. He loved Reynard, and if He took Reynard, he was His to take. I ended my prayer with, "Father, if you leave him here, I will not complain about whatever I have to do, and if you take him, I know his work here on earth was done. Whatever you do, Lord, I trust you and I thank you in advance." Years of having suffered from this man taught me if God couldn't do it, no one else could, and during the most trying moment of my life, I realized God was still in charge.

I also realized that yet again the enemy was after my faith, but oh so sad for him, I had and still have FAITH. It is easy to get sidetracked by thinking we are in control of our own fate. It is also easy to think what we experience is all about us. Sometimes God will allow us to go through some things just so the Jackies in the world can see that in the saddest of situations, her friend still has enough sense to call on the Lord.

Just when we thought things couldn't get worse, we found out differently. Now, my husband was at the LSU Health Science Center—same place, worse circumstances, and all I could do was the same thing I did before, TRUST GOD! No medical insurance, no money, bills, and an upcoming women's conference.

Now, any sane person would have canceled the conference; I am not sane!

My husband was in the ICU, and those of you who know anything about hospitals know that in ICU there are visiting times. I volunteered at the hospital he was in as a chaplain and knew they were strict about visiting hours. So this insane faith walker figured, I'd rather be at church praising the God who gave Scroggins to me than sitting at a hospital clock watching. Baby, we went to church, and I promise you…we had CHURCH!

I often go back to look at the pictures from that conference. I was snapping away, and for those of you who do not believe in angels, after you see those pictures, you will. In some pictures, you can see one person clearly while the next person is smeared by what appears to be a shadow in front of them. When I tell you we praised the Lord in that house, you had better believe we did. Pastor Karen Anderson from Mississippi came in the house with this, "Folks saying Scroggins is still alive BUT GOD; well I want people to know it ain't BUT GOD, it's JUST GOD!"

The room erupted! She gave us all our new mantle of praise: JUST GOD! The room had some of the strongest women of prayer ever assembled, and Carolyn. I single her out for a reason.

These women, along with the other women in this house (WODFLC- Word of Deliverance Family Life Church), made Thursday night worship about God and God alone! When I tell you we prayed and worshiped God as though He was sitting in the Pastor's chair weighing our worship as the sweetest aroma. When you truly love God and can worship Him despite your situation, He will take the deepest of your desires into consideration. It took FAITH to get me in the house and to keep me with my PRAISE. I often think, what if Scroggins would have died? Would I still have done what I did? I can't tell you the answer to that because only God knows. What I know is even when it could go either way, I found God worthy to be praised.

I promised myself that in order to completely liberate myself from this moment in time, I would write about it only once. Someone out there is facing his or her worst processing moment, as this was mine. It is my prayer that you've already read something that makes you desire to put your big girl panties on and keep moving. I tell my girls often, it's time to stop crying and put your big girl panties on.

So be it when your heart isn't right, it will cause you to experience some uncomfortable moments in life. I know you are saying, Danyelle, what does underwear have to do with anything? Your underwear is like your heart. If you don't have the right kind on, it can be the most uncomfortable feeling you'll ever have. So be it when your heart isn't right, it will cause you to experience some uncomfortable moments in life.

When I tell them to put their big girl panties on, I'm simply saying put on contentment and trust the process with ease. Stop whining and start praising the God who can bring you through…and we all know when things are comfortable in our lives, we praise God with ease. Well, I want them to know the same ease you praise with when things are right, mimic that when things are all wrong.

Yes, it would be easy for me just to say, "Now, now baby, stop crying." I'm not that type of mother, and they are not that type of children. They expect me to be real and to encourage them by bringing the God who created us all into the picture. I do not care what you are going through; if you bring God into the picture, it looks better, baby. Some things He allows to be thrown into your process probably came because of something you spoke. Yeah, I said it!

Your mouth has the potential to pull a hedge down, open a

hedge up, or destroy your hedge altogether. What do I mean? I'm glad you were thinking to ask. The words you speak during your process can make or break you. Words like, "How much more, Lord?" "Every time I turn around, here comes something else." "I can't win for losing." "This situation is about to kill me." "This thing is about to destroy me." If you have made any of these statements, you have caused your very own hedge of protection to be tampered with. My old Baptist church sang a stanza to an old song that said, "When I can't say anything, I'll just wave my hand." Sometimes, when we are in the middle of our process, we need to just shut up and start waving.

Waving keeps you from saying something the enemy can use against you that can impede upon your process. The devil is waiting the very moment you lay down your faith and pick up fear. When the tables turn, he will take your very words to your God to petition Him concerning your life.

If you truly come to grips with this, you will be careful of words. I often pray this prayer...Father, I ask you to destroy every assumption and acquisition that the enemy has presented You with concerning me and forgive me for every unfruitful, unnecessary, untruthful, ungodly, and unholy word that I've spoken over my life on this day. The Bible says, "Life and death are in the power of the tongue, and those who love it will eat its fruit" (Proverbs 18:21).

Here's something else I have discovered. God really does inhabits the praises of His people. If you praise God during the hard moments of your process, it speeds the delivery of your promise. Think about the postal services. If you want to get your package sooner than later, you sow a seed. That cost to overnight your package or one day it, is the seed you sow to insure you have a quicker delivery.

I hope you already sense where I'm headed? If you sow a praise seed to God, whatever promise you are standing in faith for...gets a sooner delivery date. I can't see it coming through the system. Don't know how many stops God has to hand out before mine. Could be a delay involved in the transference. None of that bothers me, because I found out if I praise God, He has the right of regulations to bring my package from the back to the front of the line.

Walk through the fire and by all means...be faithful and praise your God, because your breakthrough is waiting for your faith act. Dance Children Dance. Dance like David danced.

## LET'S PROCESS

*Philippians 4:6-8 (NASB)*

*"Be anxious for nothing, but in everything by prayer and supplication with thanksgiving let your requests be made known to God. And the peace of God, which surpasses all comprehension, will guard your hearts and your minds in Christ Jesus. Finally brethren, whatever is true, whatever is honorable, whatever is right, whatever is pure, whatever is lovely, whatever is of good repute, if there is any excellence and if anything worthy of praise, dwell on these things.*

# NOTES

## CHAPTER 12
## UNWAVERING FAITH IN THE STORM

The very day the conference ended, which was a Saturday, was the very day they moved Scroggins to a regular room. My sister-in-law was a nurse on the floor he was being transferred to, and they put him in a private room with a private shower. For those who know anything about favor, it's not always fair, but it belongs to the saints. God allowed favor to cover us. Just having my very own private shower was a blessing indeed.

My life was about to be processed in a way I'd never imagined, but once again, I felt the peace of God all over me. The same cousin Scroggins and I visited on the day of his wreck died. I tried to keep him from all outside knowledge, but it's hard when people think they have news to share. Man, did the devil try me? I almost got to where I said, "NO VISITORS ALLOWED." It was as if they weren't considering the fact that Scroggins was fighting for his life; they just had death news to share as another cousin died the same week. After Scroggins heard about these deaths, his blood pressure rose.

I petitioned God for directives, and the Lord said, "Control the atmosphere." I started playing spiritual music, which calmed him tremendously. To this day, Scroggins has a need for music; he doesn't take a shower without his spiritual music now. When his blood pressure finally stabilized, he swelled. Lord, I was all alone most days and just wanted to cry. You know people will say they will be there, but soon they forget about you. Then the Lord will put you on the heart and mind of the one who you need the most.

Scroggins' countenance would go up and down. One minute he'd be fine, and the next he'd be silently sad. I remember going into the shower and crying my eyes out, fixing my face, and coming back out ready to pretend all was well. The doctors were saying he might not regain mobility like normal, but Scroggins was having dreams of walking. We knew God was giving us confirmation in the middle of the process, and we believed the report of the Lord.

One night, deep in prayer, the Lord told me to read Proverbs 18:14. I've been up and down throughout this Bible, but I'd never seen this scripture as I did that night. He said to me, "You have to pray for his spirit and in the spirit." I stopped praying what I thought were earnest, sincere prayers and began to pray in the spirit with my spiritual language.

My husband needed what was spiritual to revive his spirit, which was battling brokenness. When you believe and trust God, He will give you a right-now solution to your right-now circumstance. All you have to do is put your trust and keep your trust in Him. Then God started sending men of God with words of prayer. I have never seen as many pastors as I did during our situation who cared. These men showed up for my husband and me, and most of them came sowing seeds. God will do it, sometimes in unfavorable circumstances.

I often tell the story that throughout all that happened, I shall never forget spending my birthday, December 26, looking out the window of the hospital at rain. I was turning 39, and it felt like time was standing still. My children brought me a birthday cake, and Mother Eunice Johnson brought me a homemade pound cake to the hospital. I cry now, thinking how those closest to me wanted me to feel special, even in my pain. God cares about you, and He sees and knows what you are going through.

It's never over until God says it's over, so we need to fast and pray. To the doctors and medical staff, things looked bleak. Doctors receive education and are required to rely on their visual observations to guide their diagnoses. Kingdom Children understand we walk by FAITH and not by SIGHT. What we see is not always the finality of what our God will do. He was and still is a miracle worker. As I mentioned, God kept giving Scroggins a recurring dream of him walking.

By this, He was aligning Scroggins' faith to exercise above what he saw in the physical, to what He was showing in the realm of dreams. I don't care what anyone tells you about your situation. You need to keep seeking God and find out what God says. I'll write this into your heart one more time: it is not over until God says it's over! I feel led to go here...you have to close your eyes to what you see, looking above unto Jesus. Hebrews 12:2 says it like this, "Looking unto Jesus the author and finisher of our faith; who for the joy that was set before him endured the cross, despising the shame, and is set down at the right hand of the throne of God."

When I keep my eyes on Jesus, I remember who He really is and what He can do for me in the confines of His will. He told me He would withhold nothing from those who walk upright, and when I look to Him, I am looking to His Word.

I've learned that when God is processing you, you must remain focused on Him...not your situation, not your circumstance, not your financial, physical, or intellectual capabilities, but on Jesus. Your eyes must remain firmly on the one who can sustain and keep you until the end of your life. I have received a new perspective on death. Why? I realize we see things one way, but only a few have ever died and known or claimed to know what happens at the point of death. If we believe the Word, it tells us when we are absent from this body, we are present with the Lord.

LET'S PROCESS

How did the author's faith help her cope with the emotional and physical challenges during Scroggins' hospitalization?

Why is it essential to trust in God's plan even when the situation seems bleak or uncertain?

What steps did the author take to create a positive and calming environment for Scroggins?

How can controlling the atmosphere around you impact the healing and recovery process?

How did the community of pastors and friends provide support during the author's difficult time?

In what ways can prayer and the support of a faith community strengthen one's resolve during trials?

LET'S PROCESS

Why is it important to keep your eyes on Jesus during challenging times?

How does focusing on Jesus and His promises help navigate through life's storms?

## CHAPTER 13
## THE REFINING FIRE OF FAITH

While Scroggins and I were in the hospital, I talked to God a lot. You better believe me. There were days when I had no calls or visitors, and after day twelve, that became alright with me. I started wanting rest time during the day. When he slept, I wanted to sleep. It was like having a baby. You know if you don't sleep when the baby sleeps, you can cancel Christmas. This was the same way. During the day, he slept, but at night, he was so uncomfortable or agitated. It got better after the Lord told me about the music, but whenever he needed to go to the bathroom, I had to get help.

One night, I asked God to give me a scripture to align our faith with. When you are seeking answers from God, try this; I promise He will give you His Word to back His heart concerning you. God gave me Romans 8:18, which reads, "For I reckon that the sufferings of this present time are not worthy to be compared with the glory which shall be revealed in us."

When you understand your latter will be greater than your former, you can rejoice in what is coming. I was speaking to a dear friend of mine, and she said she could finally see her latter would be greater than her past. It's like looking towards your future and finally seeing all the suffering you endured is paying off. There's nothing like the joy of knowing that God preserved you through your pain so you can rejoice in your future!

I felt God was saying, "Danyelle, when this is all over, folks who have seen you suffer will know that it was because of my grace and mercy you made it through. They will see my glory through you. They will see the Kingdom of your God through you and in you." You will never know the joy of being used by God unless you accept your process as prosperity in motion. It's that feeling when you don't have prosperity yet, but you feel it is coming. You don't know where it's coming from, but you believe with all your heart it's coming. When you are being processed, instead of sulking in that "why me" cheer, act like you know prosperity is coming.

Know that it is not always financial prosperity, either. The scripture says, "Beloved, I wish above all things that thou mayest prosper and be in health, even as thy soul prospereth." (3 John 1:2)

Soul prosperity is coming; to know the Lord our God as the keeper and preserver of your soul. It's knowing with every fiber of your being that you can trust God.

When you think of your health, no one wants to lack prosperity in their health. Good health is prosperity, and it belongs to the people of God.

Watching my husband go through in his body was crazy. An all-around healthy man with very few flaws suddenly diagnosed with stomach ulcers, then the wreck. I could declare then and now…There Will Be Glory After This! It's profound to watch the Word you've labored in to define your moments. God will give you defining scriptures for defining moments, and if you embrace the message, He's speaking to you, you'll come away with all the encouragement you need to persevere and fight through.

One of the greatest things birthed in me during my process was a life of prayer. I prayed, but don't think because I'm a pastor that prayer comes naturally. Not all pastors pray. I know, right? Imagine the man or woman of God over you, watching over your soul, but not praying to God. I've always been the one who bombarded the throne, but not always on purpose and not enough.

I had a sporadic prayer life, like the weather. Sometimes it would be a light rain… "Lord, thank you for life, health, and strength. Lord, bless and cover my family and me. Lord, encourage the hearts of the folks at the church you've made me oversee." Then it would be a light storm… "Lord, have mercy on me according to your love and kindness. Wash my faults and forgive my sin." Then, when trouble came, it was a tornado… "Lord, I come to you this once more and again, with a bowed-down head and a humbled heart. Asking you to move as only you can move."

Sometimes now, when I look back, I know God was sitting up there tripping like, "Really. This chick got this communication thing all jacked up. Does she actually think I'm gonna answer that every now and again cry? Do she and I really have a relationship, or is she the ex THOT that got deliverance but runs away from the relationship until it's time for her to preach or when she's broke?"

I just lost somebody right there, but if I'm gonna be real, I gotta be real, and you need to know God doesn't need side chicks who treat Him like a pimp. You don't want to see Him or talk to Him until you need saving or some money. This is exactly why the process is almost killing some of you. I heard the Lord say to me, "If you really want to be in a relationship with me, you must make it a habit of communicating with me."

Your prayer life must become habitual, just like brushing your teeth, watching The Young and The Restless, or watching the 10 O'clock Nightly News. These are things you do daily, and if you are like some folks I know, if you can't catch the soaps at eleven, you record them and watch them later. Even if you schedule prayer every day at nine in the morning, when something comes up, you must still make sure you go back to it before the day is out.

We are living in some terrible times, and worrying about how you're gonna pay your bills or what you're going to eat has gotten old. If that's what you're still praying for, then your priorities aren't in order.

If you have the right priorities, God will meet your needs for food, clothing, and necessities without you even having to ask. Come now, somebody who knows kingdom priorities needs to be shouting right here! If you are a true Kingdom citizen, you know Matthew 6:33 like you know your name:

"Seek ye first the Kingdom of God and His righteousness, and all these things shall be added unto you."

A Kingdom citizen's priority is to seek God. Their second priority is to seek His righteousness, and their third priority is to pray. When you prioritize your life to encompass Kingdom business, the Lord our God will take care of your business. You don't have to worry or fret whether God will come through for you when you are in line with His will. God will also dispatch kingdom servers to come to your rescue when you have needs, and that's exactly what Carolyn Lang became to me. She was a kingdom server dispatched by God to help me care for Scroggins during the early days of his release home.

God will not allow you to carry more than you can bear, and when the load gets too heavy, He will send backup. Now, Carolyn and I were both struggling in our own way, but God saw fit for us to be each other's strength. No, we were not best friends, nor had we known each other for years... BUT God intervened! The very people you think will get into the trenches with you are sometimes the hardest to find. God will assign His very own to your case and your cause, and if you trust His choice, you will receive even greater blessings. I trusted God's choice, and this woman has become my true sister. Almost three years later, we still have an unbreakable bond.

Are things picture perfect in my life? Heck no, but one thing is for sure…I still trust God. The same God who trusted me to go through what I have gone through will be with me as I go through what I go through now. He has not, nor will He ever, change; "I am the Lord who changes not, therefore ye sons of Jacob are not consumed" (Malachi 3:6). The irony is, it took the process to produce a change in me.

This is indeed an irony because if I really tell the truth, had it not been for the processes I faced, I would have never changed. In fact, I would have never known that I needed to change. Sometimes, we can clearly see faults in others but cannot recognize them in ourselves. I believe the devil has designed blinders just to keep us from seeing our own ways. I'm laughing because I can see him asking God, "Just let me put up a smoke screen in her mind to keep her from seeing who she really is." I know it seems a mess, but that is exactly what he is, a mess with the mess.

When God processed me, there was something about the process that made me evaluate myself. Self-evaluation is one of the most necessary procedures we have that reveals our own faults and mishaps. The truth is…some of us are so faulty we cannot believe we have faults. We have embraced our faults as integral parts of ourselves that cannot or should not be changed, and we have normalized them. The process elevates us to a place of discovery and often causes us to taste our own salt.

I don't care how good food smells. If it is too salty, it tastes horrible. I said that to say…I don't care how good you look on the outside. If sin has you salty, you still taste bad.

Your prayer life, worship, marriage, and friendships are all tainted, and nothing you produce is good. But here is the good part; although salt tastes bad, it preserves. God will allow Grace to keep you alive (preserved), so you won't die in your mess. Then He will usher you towards a process that erases the blinders from your mind and causes your thoughts to turn toward the options. Change your heart and your mind.

I have since learned when God allows me to be processed, He has a plan. God knows process births purpose. He also knows I would have never realized I needed CHANGE until He made me aware of my faults through the process. When awareness arises, purpose reveals itself and cannot hide any longer.

*Keep going you are almost finished!*

*I pray you've gotten something so far and I hope you've been encouraged right now to keep reading!*

**Jeremiah 29:11** *(NASB)*

*"For I know the plans that I have for you, declares the Lord, plans for welfare and not for calamity to give you a future and a hope."*

What scripture can you align your faith with during difficult times, and how does it help you persevere?

How did the author's prayer life evolve during the process?

Why is it important to have a consistent and sincere prayer life, especially during challenging times?

What does Matthew 6:33 teach about Kingdom priorities, and how can applying this verse transform your life?

How can focusing on seeking God and His righteousness alleviate worries about daily necessities?

How did Carolyn Lang's support demonstrate God's provision during a difficult time?

Why is it crucial to trust God's choice of people He places in your life during times of need?

How did the process of self-evaluation help the author recognize her faults and areas needing change?

In what ways can embracing the process lead to personal and spiritual growth?

What role did the author's unwavering faith play in navigating through her husband's health crisis?

How can maintaining faith in God's plan help you endure and overcome life's challenges?

# NOTES

## CHAPTER 14
## EMBRACING THE PROCESS FOR PURPOSE

For most people, after they go through a grueling process, purpose just falls into their laps. Meaning… as soon as they go through what seemed to be the hardest era of their lives, they come out doing some great things. I remember, at the beginning of my process, I was four years into the mortgage business, with more than one book on my hard drive, and no aspirations of becoming a full-time pastor or writer. My sole purpose for living was to make more money and leave a legacy of smart children on the earth. Never mind that God had more in mind for me.

Have you ever searched high and low or wondered exactly what your purpose is here on earth? For some, the thought never crosses their minds, while others toil over it with drooling hours of agony. Then there are those of us who go through some rough stuff and just land in our place called purpose.

I remember years ago when my pastor, Authur Washington, called me on a Sunday morning. He said before I went to Sunday school, he needed to see me in his office. My first thought was that I had done something wrong and was about to be reprimanded. Unbeknownst to me, God was preparing me to receive the seed of my purpose. The conversation went like this:

"Daughter, today I'm releasing you." "Pastor, what do you mean? Are you putting me out of the church?" "God told me you need to walk in your calling, and if I didn't release you, you'd never move." "Pastor, I'm waiting on Reynard." "Who said God didn't call you to pastor? Do what God desires of you to do."

I sat there and cried like a baby. Then he had someone bring Reynard in. You'll never know how hurt I was because I took it as if he was rejecting me, but he was redefining my cause. Guess what? I left and still went under the pastoral leadership of Reynard. Now, if you talked to my husband, he had no qualms with me walking as a pastor, but in the back of my head were all the men I had heard say, "God hadn't called women to preach."

I worked diligently as the co-pastor and was mighty fine right there. As soon as I became comfortable, that's when trouble broke loose. I am reminded right here of Jeremiah 1:5: "Before I formed you in the womb I knew you, and before you were born I consecrated you; I have appointed you a prophet to the nations."

It is so easy for us to decide what we want to do with our lives without even consulting God, and it is also easy for us to determine what we will not do. Not always because we feel we cannot do it, but because someone else may have determined there was no need for us to do that thing. We can believe with every fiber of our being that we are in control, but I can assure you this day, God has the last say.

When God has gifted you for a particular cause, He is going to get whatever He has purposed in you out of you. I believe we are not gifted for NOTHING! When God puts a gift in you, He also puts a work in you. You never exercise the gift if you do not work, and you never fulfill the desire of God for your life if you do not embrace the gift. With the gift comes responsibility. Look at Luke 12:48: "But he that knew not, and did commit things worthy of stripes, shall be beaten with few stripes. For unto whomsoever much is given, of him shall be much required: and to whom men have committed much, of him they will ask the more."

The more gifted God has made you, the more Kingdom responsibility you have upon the earth. Kingdom citizens have an obligation to fulfill upon the earth, and our gifts make it easy for us to carry out our assignments. When you negate the gift, you negate your assignment. It is just that simple. Some of us are actively ignoring our natural abilities. Not because we do not know they exist, but because we do not feel worthy enough to have them or comfortable enough to use them. Let me assure you this day, you will never discover your authentic place of comfort until you operate in the place God ordained.

I can remember from the time I was twelve years old, I was ministering to a married woman about her relationship.

Who at twelve knows anything about relationships? I had a gift in marriage and relationships, but that still did not stop me from having or taking part in many failed relationships. Through many failed relationships, I learned and gained knowledge that I could contrast to God's Word, and then He stabilized me in a relationship. My God, this day!

If you are reading this book and you embrace your problem as your process, you may just see your purpose shining through like a midnight star. Through all the processes in my life, I can tie each one back to who I am as a pastor. It always amazes me when I am counseling someone who is going through something I went through as a teenager. WOW!

I need you to get this right here…you can keep bucking against your purpose, and you will forever remain in a broken process. Earlier, I said that I am still being processed, but I thank God I am no longer crying about not having food or clothing. Some things get old, baby; and when you never advance through a certain process, you will only get so far until that same situation pulls you back in again. Now that I truly understand how all things work together for my good, I have made my process easier.

God does not have to use lack anymore to cause me to understand my purpose as a kingdom giver and sower. I get it! God does not have to use a failed relationship to cause me to understand Kingdom forgiving. I get it! Do you see what I am trying to say to you? As you gain wisdom and knowledge from the process, you have ways to make your purpose sustainable and solid.

When I was a teenager, my lovely momma would summon me to dish duty. Now, I don't know any young girl who likes to wash dishes after the age of seven. At first, playing in the water was fascinating, but after you get over the water fascination, dish duty is horrible. Well, I would, as she says, "half do" the dishes. Spot checks would not go great at all, and as good as Mommy would have it, she would pull all the dishes out of the cabinet and make me redo them all. She did this not one time, but every time she found that I half did the job.

I couldn't see then what I see now. Then, I saw red flags, and Mommy was waving the flag, and I was the bull who wanted to charge her but knew if I did, I would be a broke bull. Now, I see how Mommy had the same idea as God. You will go through the process repeatedly until you master and perfect what you are given to do, as God intends. Sometimes revisiting the process was worse than just getting a spanking. This leads me to 1 Peter 5:10: "And after you have suffered a little while, the God of all grace, who has called you to his eternal glory in Christ, will himself restore, confirm, strengthen, and establish you."

After I kept going through the same process, I finally realized if I just did the dishes right the first time, I wouldn't have to do them over, plus an extra load. Mommy was purposing me to be a mommy who could feed her family on a clean dish, in a clean kitchen, and with love. She was birthing purpose in me; how a Kingdom daughter who becomes a wife is supposed to do. I couldn't see it then, but I thank God for it now.

You better clap your hands right here for all the things

God allowed you to revisit repeatedly until He birthed purpose in you! Are you glad you kept going to jail until you got it? Some of us get it on the first go-around, but others (hardheaded like Mommy calls them) have to go through a thing more than once to embrace it. Whether you are a one-timer or a two or three-timer, it depends solely on your capacity to embrace the fact from the failure.

Purpose costs! If you are living out your purpose, your testimony will reveal your process cost you some sleepless nights, some tears, some friends, even some family members, some money, some houses, and even, in our case, some j...but God is still faithful. You may have to keep going through the same things repeatedly, but when you give up the process, you give up the promise. I had to preach a couple of weeks ago, and when I preached on the promises of God, I realized something. I realized that the promises of God are only for those who master the process. Scared people give up, but fighting folk stay with the process despite the pain and hurt they endure.

They endure until the end and never reach the end until they have accomplished all their purpose required them to fulfill on earth.

Folks who understand how faithful God is get up from their process (with scars and all), but they keep it moving. I'm not always invited to the parties or book events. I don't have an enormous group of friends calling me. Likes on social media are few. I have embraced purpose, and none of that bothers me. The less I have to deal with folks, the more time I have to exercise and advance my purpose. But get this, I had to learn that I can't win souls avoiding them. (Someone is going to catch that.)

You understand that when you are gifted and have a purpose, part of your process requires letting go of some things you used to do and people you used to deal with. Not everyone is fit to go through the process with you or stick around while you go through it. Hallelujah, anyhow! When you cannot go into the trenches with me, it means you will interrupt my flow, and I don't know about you, but I do not need any hindrances right now in my life. It requires changing your mind and your ways. I understand why the writer in Joel said (3:10; KJV): "Let the weak say, I am strong."

When you decide your problem is your process, you will see this life-changing ordeal differently. You will get your mind right! Yes, I said that. How? Amid your process, you'll be thinking about what God is trying to cause you to see, what you will gain from it, and where you will go after it. Through it all, keep your mind stayed on God. Isaiah 26:3 (KJV) says, "Thou wilt keep him in perfect peace, whose mind is stayed on thee: because he trusteth in thee."

Reaching purpose requires focus, and the ability to keep your mind stayed on Jesus. When all hell is breaking loose in your life, your mind still has to remain on Jesus. When your heart is heavy and the pain seems unbearable, you still have to keep your mind stayed on Jesus. I can imagine when the cross was before Him (Jesus), He had to keep His mind focused on His Father and His mission. When your mind is on your Father and your mission, God will see you through.

It was not ironic that even at the door of His death, Christ asked His Father if there was any other way to complete the task (can this cup pass? ). Sometimes I even asked, "God, could my process be lighter?" I realized, just as Christ did, not my will, but God's will be done. I can only see what is right in front of me, but God saw at the moment of my creation what I needed to accomplish on the earth as a Kingdom citizen. He knew exactly what my contribution would be. He also knew the necessary process for me to fulfill the job. Hallelujah!

LET'S PROCESS

Can you relate to a time in your life when you felt you were being "processed" or tested repeatedly? How did it impact your growth?

How do you perceive the idea that God uses challenges and repeated lessons to teach us our purpose?

In what ways do you agree or disagree with the statement: "Purpose costs"? Provide examples from your own life.

The author mentions that not everyone is fit to go through the process with you. How have you experienced this in your journey?

How can you apply the author's insights on purpose and process to your current life situation?

LET'S PROCESS

What are some practical steps you can take to focus on your mission and keep your mind stayed on God, especially during tough times?

Discuss the metaphor of the bull and the red flag in the context of resisting personal growth. How does this metaphor enhance your understanding of the author's message?

Evaluate the role of discipline (as described in the dish duty example) in achieving one's purpose. How does this compare to other forms of learning and growth?

Examine the concept of "process" as it is used in the chapter. How does this concept relate to broader themes in religious or self-help literature?

# NOTES

## CHAPTER 15
## PURPOSE BIRTHS PROMISE

I want you to understand that it is not until you are fully walking in your purpose that you will see the promises of God unfold in your life. As you go through the process, you will see the purpose of your life; and as you operate in your purpose, the promises of God will manifest, causing you to consider yourself a success.

Having a lot of money, a big house, or a nice car is not the only sign of a successful life. Some people are very successful, and the only thing they have to show for it is their faithful walk with God and their faith. So please don't get it twisted; there are some people with the evidence of a successful life whose lives are full of chaos and misery. A godly successful life is one that is full of contentment, love, and faith. It is also a life that is fully invested in kingdom concepts and is full of the favor of God. We say it all the time, "Favor is better than money." I wonder if we truly believe it.

There was a woman by the name of Minister Linda Baldwin, whom the Lord put into my life. I called her Mudear after some time, and I remember being drawn to her from the moment we met. She didn't have money, her name wasn't on books, nor was she known around the world, but this, my friend, was a successful woman. Mother Linda learned how to live a life of faith, and at the end of her life, she became my superstar. Not because of worldly indications of a successful life, but because of the spiritual indications of a faithful, prayerful life that abounded in the favor of God.

I was just speaking with a young woman who Mother Linda also touched, and I found out she had been talking to some other ladies who were declaring just as we were. Mother Linda had so much faith in God and trusted Him with her everything. As a junior minister, I could have aspired to become like some of the global evangelists and pastors, but I aspired to be like a little woman named Minister Linda Baldwin.

Mother Linda might have believed that her only purpose on earth was to be the mommy of her son and stepsons and take care of the many daycare children as she was degreed to do, but God had more in mind. She had gone through many processes, and as she pushed through, her humility became impeccable and the favor over her life became extremely noticeable. She completed her assignment and pushed through until the end.

I must revisit the birthing process...

As you are being processed, you must complete the task and push through to the end. No woman ever gets on the birthing table and just declares in the middle of labor that she's tired and going to give up. In case she clunks out (for lack of a better word), the doctors are going to get that baby even if they have to cut her to get it. Some of you have clunked out. You have decided that the process hurts too much to go any further, and if the anointing costs this much, you don't even want it.

I hate to break the news to you, but purpose has to come forward through you, even if God has to cut it out.

My God, today! Giving up is not something you are able to do. You were not supposed to allow situations to go unfinished. You were meant to persevere. How do I know this? God would have never put purpose in you if the process killed, destroyed, broke, or caused you to accept failure and defeat. That is why often in the Old Testament, God would send the Israelites to battle, and instead of them having to fight, He would declare that the battle belonged to Him. Yes, it is you facing the process (the fight), but it is the Lord our God who is going to fight the battle for you in the middle of your process. He sent this word specifically in Isaiah 54:17: "No weapon that is formed against thee shall prosper; and every tongue that shall rise against thee in judgment thou shalt condemn. This is the heritage of the servants of the Lord, and their righteousness is of me, saith the Lord."

If you open your heart and mind to receive this today, you will see just how powerful, resilient, and tenacious you are. You will also better understand that although the process feels like weaponry, it might cut you, but it will not kill you. It might sting you, but it will not break you. It might even make you cry, but it will never cause you to die.

Even in the midst of the birthing process, when you are worn out, you can always hear the best word you have ever heard: PUSH. For some of you, the end of this processing period is almost over. Any day now, the Lord is going to usher you to PUSH, but whatever you do, do not push too soon. I remember when I was pregnant with DJ, and the nurse wanted me to wait for Dr. Chitham. She said, "Please don't push."

The pressure was the most intense pressure I'd ever been under. I screamed, "I can't keep him."

Some of us prematurely push through the process, and it does not develop us the way God intended it to. We never get the fullness of the process because our minds are constantly awaiting the PUSH. We can't see the beauty or the blessing in the pregnancy (the process) because we focus too much on the end results or lack the patience to let time build strength. God desires to take you to another level in Him, and with each level requires a certain magnitude of strength. The process is the only way for you to gain this strength, and you will only recognize the promises of God when you embrace the purpose of your life.

Oh my! I heard it in my spirit… "But when is this crap going to be over?" "Haven't I already been through enough stuff?" "I'll be glad when I see my morning." Don't get me wrong, it's okay to be ready, but just because you're ready doesn't mean God is ready. Even when I go back in my mind to when I was pregnant, not only was I ready for the baby to come, but I'd gotten on their father's nerves so much that he was ready too. I wrote that, so you'd consider the fact that your process does not just affect you; it affects everyone around you. That still does not give you permission to PUSH too early.

When I was pregnant with DJ, at the very beginning, the fetus was threatening to come early. I received a warning to stay in bed and keep my feet up during the early stages of my pregnancy with DJ, but I didn't follow their advice. During our process, God will send His Word specifically to us, and sometimes we ignore Him, sort of like I did with the doctor's instructions. I had a husband; I had two other babies, and I didn't have time to be lying around in bed all day.

Have you ever been in the middle of a process, and God sends word for you just to pray? Everything in your spirit tells you to pray. You wake up at the strangest times, like He's pulling you to converse with Him. You feel the longing or desire to pray, but. There's always a "but" trying to wreck the process, and you recognize that the "but" is never bigger than the promise; not even your "butt." I said a mouthful right there…at least I think I did. I can look back in my life and see how I always had a but for my obedience to God.

But I don't have the money, Lord. But I don't feel worthy, Lord. But I'm not good enough, Lord. But I wasn't born COGIC. But I can't sing like most people. But how will I do that, Lord? But I don't know how to start that business. But I don't know how to run a church.

I can go on and on, telling you how I tried to block what God desired to do in and through me because I had my set of "buts." That's how we know we are at the door of processed completion. We want to come out, but we make all kinds of excuses for why we can't come out! God is giving us the answers we've been waiting for, but our own "buts" blind us from seeing that as long as we keep saying "but," we cannot PUSH.

Back to the pregnancy...so because the baby was threatening to come early and I would not adhere to the doctor's instructions, I ended up on an island off mainland Japan all by myself in a hospital, and one director of the hospital who was American was in the United States on leave. God, the fear I felt. I remember feeling like someone had thrown me into prison, and no one except Dwight could come to see me. I was threatening to abort the process, and in the midst of the pregnancy process, God was causing me to endure processing.

I'd always been one of those people afraid to do anything by myself. As long as I had someone with me, I was okay, but to go at it alone was so scary. God was processing me for my journey in ministry right there. Sometimes when I think about how alone I am in ministry, it's frightening; but somehow God always reminds me how He was with me on that island. He's still the same God, and He's with me now. I made it my purpose to hear Him, and being on that island taught me how to listen and hear Him. I received the assurance that when I heard Him, I should simply act on it.

God was closing me away from everything in order for me to recognize His voice. I can truly say it was through this process I found my purpose wrapped in the prophetic. I found God did not care how I lived my teenage years; He desired me. Not partial parts of me; but all of me. Yes, low down dirty me.

I pray that encourages someone! You may not feel you are worthy, but God says, "You are." He's not concerned about who you were. He knows the same strength and tenacity you used back then when you were a sinner, you'll use it to build

His Kingdom. God carefully picks kingdom ambassadors because their jobs require just a little more than that of a normal kingdom citizen. God targets them for front-line service. Often, they may not fit the typical expectations, but the fact is that they have gone through a thorough selection process for their role.

## LET'S PROCESS

What does the author suggest about recognizing one's own power and resilience during the process?

How does the metaphor of the birthing process illustrate the concept of enduring and completing one's purpose?

What lesson did the author learn from their experience of prematurely pushing through the process?

Can you recall a time when you felt like giving up in the middle of a challenging process? How did you find the strength to continue?

How do you relate to the author's struggle with making excuses ('buts') for not following through with God's plan?

## LET'S PROCESS

What are some 'buts' that you have encountered in your own life, and how have they affected your progress?

What practical steps can you take to ensure you stay focused and obedient to God's instructions during your process?

How can you develop the patience needed to see the beauty and blessings in your current process rather than just focusing on the end result?

Analyze the metaphor of the birthing process in the context of spiritual growth. How does it help convey the author's message about perseverance and faith?

Discuss the significance of the author's isolation on the island off mainland Japan. How did this period shape their understanding of listening to and obeying God's voice?

Evaluate the impact of premature actions ('pushing too soon') on personal and spiritual development. What are the potential consequences and lessons learned?

How do you interpret the author's statement, "The 'but' is never bigger than the promise"? How can this perspective change your approach to challenges?

In what ways can you find strength and assurance in the idea that God targets Kingdom Ambassadors for the front line?

LET'S PROCESS

How can you use the experiences and lessons from your past to build a stronger, more faithful future?

# NOTES

## CHAPTER 16
## WE ALWAYS SURVIVE

I can just imagine Linda sitting with the Father, talking about how she weathered her processes to reach her ultimate promise. Some will find their promises on earth, while others will attain their ultimate promise when they transition. Either way, we all should be actively doing whatever is necessary to take hold of God's promises.

You must never allow the processes to happen and only half embrace them, as if they are not your transportation to greater things. You must drive forth headstrong, determined to endure. Now, I do not want you to think that I'm making light of all the things you've had to endure and go through. For some of you, it seems like there have been so many hardships, but there is a method to this madness.

Procedures eliminate each process God will give you when you willfully embrace the evidence presented, consult God for direction, and maintain your position while you wait. When I think of how we literally moved from process to process, it seemed like we couldn't catch our breath before something else hit. Our lives were almost like being in the center of a video game—dodging bullets from enemy fire, waiting on God for the next direction, praying we don't fail, and trusting that we win either way. Some challenges were easy, while others were so hard, but we kept our minds stayed on Jesus. Even now, my mind heavily reflects upon Isaiah 26:3: "Thou wilt keep him in perfect peace, whose mind is stayed on thee: because he trusteth in thee."

No matter how many processes you face or how hard they are, if you keep your mind centered on Christ, you will have peace in the storm. Ever seen someone going through what appears to be the worst moment or event of their life, but they seem as calm as a winter's day? You've witnessed one of two types of people: one, someone who doesn't care about what's going on, or two, someone who has kept their mind stayed on God. There really is no in-between.

After eight months of being confined to a bed and a wheelchair, the therapist decided it was time to stand Scroggins up. I pushed him into the work area, and he sat answering every question. Then it was time for the big event. The therapist wrapped a harness around Scroggins' waist. One got behind him while the other stood in front. They counted and then lifted Scroggins to his feet.

I stood by in total gratefulness until Scroggins' eyes rolled back in his head, and his body went limp. I literally lost control as the therapists quickly put him on the table, one straddling him and the other lifting the table so his legs went up and his head went down. It was like watching a horror film, and I couldn't yell, "Cut!" All I could say was, "Lord, surely You have not brought us this far to allow him to die because he tried to stand up."

Sometimes, when you are down, you find out how strong your legs really are. I wrote all of that to tell you: I know sometimes it feels like you'd be better off just staying down because every time you come up, something is lurking around the corner to knock you back down. I promise you that the blessing is in repeatedly getting up, not in staying down, until you are ready to walk out of the storm. You also find out if someone around you is strong enough to carry you; keeping you company with the same mindset.

What am I talking about? I believe Shadrach, Meshach, and Abednego in the furnace together were about more than three boys who wouldn't obey the king. I believe God was showing us that when you have someone in the process with you, as long as you stick together and trust God together, not only will you weather the process, but God will get in the situation with you. When Scroggins was in that wheelchair, I was down for whatever. If I had to push him all the days of our lives…get ready, set, push, baby!

When I vowed to believe what he believed—that he would walk—no matter how the failed attempt to stand up materialized, I was going to believe in the power of our God and stay right there with my pair of good legs until God got in the furnace with us. It's so important to know who is on your team. You must know if you have like-minded people in your bed and in your life. Folks who buck against your God will always buck against your faith in your God and in yourself. When the people closest to you oppose you, it is hard to keep your mind stayed on God and your faith elevated to your fullest potential in God. Therefore, you ought to be marrying a mate because you have found someone to touch and agree with, not someone just to sleep with. You also need friends who have experienced testing and trials in the things of Christianity. Therefore, when you are in a process, you will have someone encourage you in the things of the Lord and in the Word of the Lord.

Three weeks after the failed attempt to stand up, we were at home, sitting in our bedroom. Scroggins, at the foot of our bed in the hospital bed, turned and looked at me and said, "Baby, I want to stand up." My stomach almost hit the floor, but my instinct said, "Let's do this." I stood up, called our cousin Tarus (so I'd have support and help), tied a huge belt around his waist, and prepared for the best.

I knew two things: God had not brought us this far to leave us, and Scroggins had already received the revelation of him walking. The Bible says, "There's no good thing He will withhold from them who walk upright."

When we live according to the Word of God and stay in the Will of God, it does not matter how many processes we face or how hard they are; we will survive and come out on top. For those who may not know, Scroggins made four steps forward that day and four steps back to his bed. He was so tired afterward, but he did not pass out. It was indeed the day I truly realized what a miracle he was. But had Scroggins not made one step, I would still have believed in the due process of the process. I know you are wondering what is due process of the process. In the next chapter, you will find out. Keep going but process before you continue.

LET'S PROCESS

What does the author suggest about embracing the processes in life fully?

How does the author describe the nature of life's hardships and the way they seem to come one after another?

What is the significance of keeping one's mind stayed on Jesus, according to the author?

Have you ever felt like you were constantly moving from one hardship to another? How did you cope with it?

Can you think of a time when you had to support someone else through their process? How did it affect your own faith and perseverance?

LET'S PROCESS

How do you maintain your focus and peace in the midst of life's storms?

What can you do to identify and eliminate the negative influences in your life that hinder your faith?

How can you support someone else in their process while maintaining your own faith and perseverance?

Discuss the importance of having like-minded individuals in your life during difficult processes. How does this impact your ability to persevere?

Evaluate the author's use of biblical stories to illustrate their points. How effective are these references in enhancing the narrative?

How can you use the experiences and lessons from your past processes to build a stronger, more faithful future?

What steps can you take to better recognize and embrace God's voice and direction in your life, even during difficult times?

# NOTES

## CHAPTER 17
## DUE PROCESS OF PROCESS

This is an administration of the law of process. It is not permissible for anyone to deny an individual their spiritual right to remain in a process for as long as they need or until they have gained what is required. All processes must conform to one's own ability to bear, accepting God's hedge of protection principles as the right of the one processed to confer with the Processor (God) and defy the accuser (the Devil).

You may remain in a process as long as you desire. It's possible to decide that you don't want to go through it and simply quit, but it will resurface as you possess the ability to overcome. You can have discussions, exchange thoughts, consult with, or simply talk to God while you are being processed. Last, you can defy the one who wanted the process to destroy you, break you, turn you away from God, and kill you by determining that you will go through it and not die.

WOW! I hope you got that, because I sure did. I have

rights, and I will use every right I have for the betterment of who I am. No matter what God allows me to be processed with, I am convinced that nothing shall by any means harm me or separate me from His (Christ) love. It wasn't until I got to this point that I fully understood where Paul was coming from in Romans 8:35-39 (NASB):

"Who will separate us from the love of Christ? Will tribulation, or distress, or persecution, or famine, or nakedness, or peril, or sword? Just as it is written, 'For Your sake we are being put to death all day long; we were considered as sheep to be slaughtered.' But in all these things we overwhelmingly conquer through Him who loved us. For I am convinced that neither death, nor life, nor angels, nor principalities, nor things present, nor things to come, nor powers, nor height, nor depth, nor any other created thing, will be able to separate us from the love of God, which is in Christ Jesus our Lord."

Paul starts by asking who shall separate us and then, in the same verse, asks what shall separate us from the love of Christ. You know that no matter who or what—whether person or situation—nothing we experience has the authority to break our connection with Christ. Hallelujah! Baby, that's a praise moment right there.

As you go through the process, your love for Christ should deepen with each victory! When God finds you fit to be processed, He gives you a distinct opportunity to move beyond where you are right now (in relationship with Christ) and who you are right now (as a child of Christ). All people experience processes, but not all understand they move them forward in life and closer to God. Why? Because God knows, just like you know, that some people are happy right where they are. He lets the devil keep them blind until they are fully ready to accept being able to see. Will you allow this book to help you see?

See what, Pastor Danyelle? That your life is so much more than getting married, having children, going to church, going to work, going to school, coming back home to watch a little television, cooking a little meal, and going to bed to start all over week after week. Being processed gives you exposure to elevation, and when God is elevating you, He is positioning you for kingdom work on a kingdom level. The greater your processing is, the greater your work is. So what you are looking at as "so many and so hard," God is saying, "So much for someone so capable," because to whom much is given, much is required (Luke 12:48)!

Now I have to be real: no one could have beaten me saying, "Lord, if I have to go through all of this, I don't want it," but there is nothing like the feeling I have when I preach in a room full of women, and years or sometimes months later, I hear, "I was delivered that night when you brought the Word." Sometimes I feel like God is sitting on the throne when I so humbly say, "To God be the glory," chuckling at me. He knows that the processing I went through was necessary for me to be as effective as He desired me to be.

Although it's never for me to get His glory, it feels good to know He processed me to be used for Kingdom work and to be effective as I'm used. Do you get it now? Can you now embrace your process as your come-up instead of as your breakdown?

## LET'S PROCESS

What is the significance of having the right to remain in a process according to the author?

How does the author explain the concept of overcoming the accuser (the Devil) during the process?

What lesson does the author draw from Romans 8:35-39 about separation from the love of Christ?

Have you ever felt like giving up during a difficult process? How did you find the strength to continue?

Can you think of a time when you felt your connection with Christ deepened through a challenging process?

How do you perceive the role of hardships in your spiritual growth and relationship with God?

LET'S PROCESS

What practical steps can you take to consult with God and seek His guidance during your current process?

How can you develop a mindset that views challenges as opportunities for growth rather than setbacks?

What can you do to strengthen your faith and trust in God's plan, especially during tough times?

Evaluate the author's use of personal anecdotes and biblical references to illustrate their points. How effective are these elements in enhancing the narrative?

In what ways can you find strength and assurance in the idea that God is with you during your trials?

How can you use the experiences and lessons from your past processes to build a stronger, more faithful future?

# NOTES

CHAPTER 18

THE TESTIMONY

Have you ever shared your testimony with someone, and right before your eyes, their expression changes from that of a defeated foe to a strengthened warrior? I believe that when we commit to sharing the processes we go through, we also commit to something or someone beyond ourselves. Thus, not only do we become over-comers because of our testimony, but others do as well.

So, what is it about our process that gives us a testimony and brings glory to God? My grandmother used to say, "Until you truly understand where you came from, you will never know the value of where you are now." Think about that. When I sit down and carefully consider where I was a few years ago versus where I am now, I know with no doubt that there is a God and He is working on my behalf. Even when I think of Scroggins lying in those hospital beds versus where he is now, I know God deserves glory, honor, and praise.

Our process was great, but it was never greater than the glory God received after we went through it. I can remember the first Sunday I wheeled Scroggins into New Vessels Ministries. The people were just amazed. He still had no ability to walk, but just the fact he could sit was exceptional but crazy! When I think back, I just shake my head because God knew.

Upon getting ready to leave the hospital, we knew that in less than ten days, I'd have to get him back to the hospital. He still had a bar in his leg, and it was only he and I. I called around, and no one had a wheelchair except his now-deceased Aunt Julie. I borrowed her wheelchair, and it was the worst trip I ever took. He kept sliding out of the seat because the chair was too small, and the way his leg had to be propped—I cringe even now. I kept pulling him up, and my poor arms were already aching from getting him into the borrowed vehicle to get him to the hospital. Did you see that? I even had to borrow a vehicle to get him there because 1) the wreck destroyed our vehicle and 2) even if it hadn't, he wouldn't have been able to ride in the backseat of a car.

Well, I called our angels on earth and explained I had to do something different. I asked the doctor for a wheelchair prescription, and he was astonished that the hospital hadn't given us one when Scroggins was discharged. After I got him back home, I set out to find a wheelchair that would not only fit but would help me. Was God in the process? You better believe He was. The store I found was too costly, so I said a brief prayer in the car. Then, nobody but the Lord allowed the information from a small family owned medical supply company to pop up.

I couldn't picture the place, but I called the number anyway. A young woman answered and said, "Yes, we are right beyond the light at Kingston Road and Flournoy Lucas. Come on by; we have some in the store."

I and the church mother went to the store, and behold, there was a BMW of wheelchairs. This thing did everything except eject the person out of it. It had a back that would recline into a semi-bed. It had leg lifts and cushions, was easy to assemble and tote, and the chair was from God on high. I knew it was because I could carry Scroggins to church and keep him comfortable for an hour and a half, all because of a perfect wheelchair. Was it expensive? Yes, but it was well worth every penny.

Some may wonder, why read a testimony about a wheelchair? Someone else might say, Lord, help me find a store where I can get this type of wheelchair for my loved one. What I'm saying is, your testimony might seem like nothing to one person, but to someone else, it is just the blessing of information they needed to make their present situation better. My God, did you catch the revelation? Testimonies have a specific purpose, at a specific time, with a specific reach. The one who shares must have faith that God would not have ushered you to share unless there was an intended purpose, an intended time, and an intended reach. He's INTENTIONAL, people, and He does everything with PURPOSE in mind!

This entire book is a big testimonial, but even more importantly, someone will miss the message while someone else will scoop it up and run with it. When I started writing this book, I was dealing with so many emotions from that period of my life that I was leery.

My grandmother, the late Thessalonian Anderson, came to my house in December 2014. No one could take her to her appointment, so my aunt called me. I never thought in a million years that Grandmother would want to stay at my house, but she kept asking my aunt about coming, so we picked her up a few days early.

We laughed at my jokes, ate dinner, snacked on many things, and I realized at one point God was giving us an opportunity to love one another. Well, I took her as scheduled to her doctor's appointment on Friday, and she remained in the ICU from Friday until Tuesday. We discovered she had cancer, and the doctors informed us she would receive hospice care. I ended up taking her to her home, but had to spend some nights and days there for handling business. On Thursday night, it was so hard for me to sleep. I just kept feeling like we weren't in the home alone. I know Jesus is always present with us when we accept Him as Lord over our lives, but I cannot truly put into words the heaviness and gratefulness mixed in one big emotion.

I texted Scroggins around one in the morning and said, "Baby, I pray Momma doesn't die on me." His exact words were, "Danyelle, the Lord knows how you feel about death, and He will not subject you to that." His words were like a weight off my shoulder, and I got this from his words: Our God knows who you are and how much you can handle. He will never put more on you than you can bear. For me, that became an opportunity for praise. I turned my Pandora on my phone to the Tamela Mann Station, and right as I turned it on, she was singing, "I Can Only Imagine." Then Bryon Courtney Wilson came on after that singing "Already Here."

It was as if Pandora was trying to explain something to me. I did not want to accept in the natural but was rejoicing over in the spirit. I worshipped, and before I knew it, the clock read 3:30.

Already a rather sleepless night, my feet hit the floor at 5:15 A.M. I started her breakfast and prepared her water for a morning bath. After I finished, I asked, "Is there anywhere in particular you want me to read for you?" When she said no, I said, "Well, let's just go over to John and see how much Jesus loves us." I began reading at John 1. Like the teacher I am, I asked Grandmother who John was talking about, and she replied, "Jesus." Then I read a little farther, and I got to the story of Nicodemus. I asked her, "Grandmother, are you born again?" She replied, "Yes, I sure am." After I finished chapter 3, someone knocked on the door. It was one of her friends, visiting her before he went to his doctor's appointment.

We had more morning visitors, and before I knew it, it was time for my aunt to come so I could go home. She did not want me to leave, but because of the long night I had, I just wanted to kiss my husband, take a long bath, and get in my bed for at least one night. I called before I lay down to check on her, and all was well. Then, thirty minutes later, I felt something almost like the same feeling I had the night before. I called again, and my aunt said her sugar was low. I asked them to call the hospice nurse and if I should come back. Of course, my aunt Faye said, "Yes."

I packed a couple more items in my already packed bag and told Scroggins, "I'm just going to move in with Grandmother until the Lord comes." He agreed and put on his shoes because he said the Spirit told him to drive me.

Gloster, where I live, is approximately thirty minutes away from my grandmother's house. I got less than ten minutes away when they called to tell me my grandmother was gone. Although I found it hard to believe, I was certain that the Lord had been in proximity. There was a presence in that house, apart from myself, that I could sense. Since I have never died, I am unaware of who comes to retrieve the children of God when they pass away; I know their spirits return to the Lord. Something compelled me to worship. I drifted off to sleep between 3:30 and 5:15, but even then, my eyes periodically popped open. It is as if the Spirit in me was aware of the Giver.

I say all this to explain that my grandmother passed away just days before my 41st birthday, but her passing made me see life differently. It was all so overwhelming! So much so that an old familiar spirit tried to invade (panic attacks), and I grieved for her properly (with tears) so I would not be subject to spiritual attacks. I also realized that God is sovereign.

I realized He could take life as He chooses, and He can set the stage for His coming as He sees fit. I realized that when He leaves a life (as with Scroggins); He leaves it with a purpose in mind. When he takes a life (as with Grandmother), he fulfills this earth's purpose completely. If my grandmother did nothing else, she birthed the Joseph in the world—Joe, who would stand as my earthly father to prevent me from being raised in a single-parent household. It was to give me my first glimpse of what a parental structure should simulate, whether healthy or unhealthy; pure or not pure. I've seen family at its best and at its worst; strong and weakened; with God and away from God.

Mainly so that my testimony would be mine, and my sharing would help someone and even me overcome! My friends, your walk in PURPOSE rewards you with a testimony that will weather the times and defend the goodness and character of your God. It was the seven days from the doctor telling my grandmother she had cancer to the seven days later when she died that made me ultimately aware of my PURPOSE. It became as if, instead of living my life as I have before, waiting on next year to do something, I'm now living in seven-day increments. What can I do in seven days to make a difference in someone's life?

This is my constant question. The Lord needed me to see His PURPOSE is sure, and our journey is riding on the realization of the revelation that it's EXCLUSIVELY Jesus. The way we get to our ultimate success, which is life with the Father, is by Jesus, who says in John 14:6, "I am the way, the truth, and the life. No one comes to the Father except through Me."

In that, we see Jesus is directional, structural, and intentional. Embracing Him allows you to flow easily into what you have been assigned to do. Don't allow anyone to tell you anything different! Education can only take you so far. Money can only take you so far. Influential and affluent connections can only take you so far. Charm and charisma can only take you so far. Talents and wisdom can only take you so far. Jesus can take you where these things and people will and can never take you. Let me encourage you to find PURPOSE, but not apart from the one who PURPOSED you.

Declare this always: Psalm 138:8 "The Lord will perfect that which concerns me; Your mercy, O Lord, endures forever; Do not forsake the works of Your hands."

# LET'S PROCESS

***Psalm 138:1-8***
*I will give You thanks with all my heart;*
*I will sing praises to You before the gods.*
*² I will bow down toward Your holy temple*
*And give thanks to Your name for Your lovingkindness and Your truth;*
*For You have magnified Your word according to all Your name.*
*³ On the day I called, You answered me;*
*You made me bold with strength in my soul.*
*⁴ All the kings of the earth will give thanks to You, O Lord,*
*When they have heard the words of Your mouth.*
*⁵ And they will sing of the ways of the Lord,*
*For great is the glory of the Lord.*
*⁶ For though the Lord is exalted,*
*Yet He regards the lowly,*
*But the haughty He knows from afar.*

LET'S PROCESS

> ⁷ Though I walk in the midst of trouble, You will ʲrevive me;
> You will stretch forth Your hand against the wrath of my enemies,
> And Your right hand will save me.
> ⁸ The Lord will accomplish what concerns me;
> Your lovingkindness, O Lord, is everlasting;
> Do not forsake the works of Your hands.

What realization did the author come to regarding God's sovereignty through the passing of her grandmother?

How does the author describe her new perspective on living life in seven-day increments?

In what ways did the author decide to grieve her grandmother's passing to avoid spiritual attacks?

What does the author mean by saying that living with purpose rewards you with a testimony that defends God's goodness and character?

How does the author's understanding of Jesus being "directional, structural, and intentional" influence her view on purpose?

Have you ever experienced a moment where sharing your testimony helped someone else? How did it make you feel?

How do you cope with the loss of a loved one, and what role does your faith play in that process?

What steps can you take to ensure you live with purpose and intention, as described by the author?

How can you support others who are going through a similar grieving process and help them find purpose?

# NOTES

## CHALLENGES: UNCOVERED OR DISCOVERED

Write the challenges that you uncovered or discovered as a result of reading this book and answering the questions...

## A WORD FROM THE AUTHOR

Dear Reader,

Thank you for picking up this book and embarking on a journey with me through the various processes of life. Writing this book has been both a deeply personal and transformative experience. It is a testament to the trials, triumphs, and revelations that have shaped my walk with God.

In sharing my stories and testimonies, my hope is to inspire and encourage you to embrace your own journey with a renewed sense of purpose. Life's challenges are not meant to break us but to build us, to draw us closer to God, and to reveal the incredible strength and resilience He has placed within each of us. As you read, I pray you find comfort in knowing that you are not alone in your struggles and that each process is a stepping stone towards greater fulfillment and understanding.

This book is more than a collection of experiences; it is a call to see beyond the immediate pain and confusion, to recognize the divine orchestration in our lives, and to trust that God's plans for us are good. Every chapter is a reminder that our trials have a purpose, and through faith and perseverance, we can emerge stronger and more aligned with our true calling.

I encourage you to take these stories to heart, reflect on your own journey, and share your testimony with others. There is power in our shared experiences, and in them, we find the strength to continue, the wisdom to grow, and the faith to believe in the promises of God.

May this book be a source of hope, encouragement, and a deeper connection with the one who PURPOSED you for greatness. Remember, every process is part of a greater plan, and with Jesus, we can navigate through anything life throws our way.

Blessings,
**Pastor Danyelle Scroggins**

## ABOUT THE AUTHOR

Danyelle Scroggins is the Senior Pastor of New Vessels Ministries in Shreveport, Louisiana. She is the author of special books like Put It In Ink, Graced After The Pain, Evonta's Revenge, & Enduring Love. She's the wife of Pastor Reynard Scroggins and the mother of three young adults: Raiyawna, Dobrielle, and Dwight Jr.. She's privilege to be the grandmother of Emiya'rai Grace & Maddox Rai.

Danyelle loves writing inspirational stories set in Louisiana, where she lives preaching, teaching, and enjoying writing by the window. Learn all about her here www.danyellescroggins.com.

Also find her on Facebook, Twitter, and Bookbub.

- facebook.com/authordanyellescroggins
- twitter.com/pastordanyelle
- bookbub.com/profile/danyelle-scroggins
- goodreads.com/danyellescroggins

SPECIAL THANKS

Hello Wonderful Reader,

I pray you've enjoyed your journey through the corners of my mind. I want to thank you for reading my books. To those who have just discovered books by ME, thank you for taking the chance on a new-to-you author.

Please take the time to leave a review.

It helps those who may like the same types of books find a new author.

Want a FREE BOOK, join my mailing list and get MORE THAN DIAMONDS.

# READ MORE THAN DIAMONDS

Today was already beginning to be a long day. It's the day before our banquet, and I've got tons of work before me. I have been up and at it for close to two hours, and it's already been draining, to say the least. I promised myself I wouldn't let the Mother's Day banquet at Faith Temple Cathedral stress me. I guess my promises aren't close to being like God's.

The blessing in this is unlike a lot of first ladies, the women at FTC like me. And, I like them. I got more than enough signatures on my list to help me pull this off. But when it came to doing things, I always rely upon my crew, which included my sisters-by-church, Stephanie and Sheila.

We have been friends since we came into the world. I can remember having parties in my backyard, and we were the only three children there. Each of us is married now, but that still doesn't stop the love nor fellowship we are accustomed to having. I still expect them to be where I am.

And like usual, they late.

I won't get mad because I'm blessed. In the last eighteen years, we've seen our babies become fine men and young women. I've seen my oldest put on what the military calls his dress whites and leave me crying like I've lost my mind. Which is why I'm hosting this banquet.

After Scott left for the military, my husband, Pastor Roderick Prince Strong, told me in the most unsettling way, "Girl, you need to find something to do."

I'm a black woman, and there are just some things you don't say to me. He got a royal tongue lashing that I had to apologize for later. That's the only thing I hate about being married to a pastor. After you tell them off, the Spirit is quick with a reminder to touch not His anointed.

That's why I am the first to tell single women or men who think they want to be married to a pastor, "Be careful what you ask for." God will remind you quickly, they belong to Him and that He's their boss.

After most warnings, I usually evaluate what hubby has said. In the case of Scott and me, he won. I'm not ashamed to say, "He was right." I needed to find something to do besides be a mother. Scott, my adopted child, lost his mother and father to domestic violence. And I think I used that to bind me so close to him. When it came time for him to leave, I nearly had a nervous breakdown.

Bad mothers don't understand that.

But good mother's—who make their families their entire life—know precisely where I'm coming from. We love all of our children, but there's something special about a mother and her son. Lora, my daughter, no one can love her more than Roderick P. Strong. The sun rises and sets on his sweet baby girl, and I hate to see that thing coming.

If she comes to me for anything, you better believe it's because she knows it's in my closet. Other than begging, she rarely pays two-cents of attention to me. But trust me when I say, I'm not jealous. It keeps her out of my pockets and in her daddy's, which is fine with me. But Scott was a whole entirely different tune.

After my baby left, I had no choice but to spend a couple days in therapy with Pastor Dr. Rosalee Day. It was so life-changing because since I married Roderick and God blessed me with Scott and Lora, I've never thought about myself.

It was nothing for me to go into Wally World with stockings and panties on the list for myself, and when I got home, I'd bought everything for everyone except me. It was the same as the grocery store. No matter how many snacks I had on the list for me, I never bought them. I'd go in the store with a budget, and after I see something that one of them would want, I start axing my list starting with my stuff.

Dr. Day showed me how what I considered as healthy mothering was abuse to myself. What good mother who puts her husband and children's needs before her own, thinks it's abuse to herself? I surely didn't. I thought I was doing exactly what the virtuous woman was doing. Nevertheless, she reminded me that the virtuous woman made herself some clothing according to scripture, and she dressed in colorful linens and silks. Pastor Day said, "And it wasn't cheap."

Of course, you know when I got home, I ran to my Bible to reread Proverbs 31. Like myself, I realized she did a lot for her family, but she didn't cancel herself out. I had a lot of thinking to do, and praying too.

I needed God's directives on becoming me. Not just a pastor's wife or mother. I cried, "Lord, teach me how to love and be me."

Thinking back, there was a time in my life when I knew what Destiny wanted. Over eighteen years and I promise that's been lost. The blueprint was in my hands, then I had children and lost those plans. I can't lay the full weight on my babies. I became a mother to many when I accepted Roderick's proposal.

I cannot count all the people at FTC who call me Mother Destiny or Momma. At first, I wanted to go around telling them just to call me Destiny. The old heads let me know that as the first lady, I was not only a mother to my own but a spiritual mother of all who called FTC their church.

And the weights got heavier.

If you'd like to continue reading More Than Diamonds, you can join my mailing list and read it for FREE!

Here's the Link: **bit.ly/3DfbLL0**

# READ MORE THAN GRATEFUL

**More Than Grateful** follows First Lady Rachel Tate as she faces the most challenging trial of her life. Married to Pastor Jonas Tate, the charismatic leader of Rise Church, Rachel is determined to make her mark by organizing her first women's conference, aptly named More Than Grateful. But the journey is anything but smooth.

As Rachel steps into her new role, she encounters resistance from the women in the congregation, particularly from Allison, who once hoped to marry Jonas herself. The tension between Rachel and Allison spills over, straining Rachel's relationship with her husband and testing her resolve. Feeling the pressure of anger, Rachel does something she soon regrets, throwing her world into turmoil.

Thankfully, Rachel is not alone. The unwavering support of two seasoned first ladies—Lady Destiny Strong of Faith Temple Cathedral and Lady Stephanie Jones of Willow Grounds Baptist Church—helps Rachel to find her footing.

These wise mentors guide her through the labyrinth of first lady responsibilities, teaching her the delicate art of leadership while preserving her own peace and purpose.

Through trials and triumphs, Rachel learns that genuine gratitude comes not from the absence of challenges but from the strength and wisdom gained in overcoming them. In the end, will Rachel's newfound understanding and the support of her friends be enough to help her rise above the trials and emerge stronger, or will one poor decision cost her everything she holds dear?

ALSO BY DANYELLE SCROGGINS

*Keatchie Corner*

POTENTIAL NEED HEALED WEAK DREAM STRUGGLE GUILTY PLENTY FOUND INTENSE

*Smith Family Cowgirls & Christian Romance*

Blame It On My Boots

*A Louisiana Finest*

Mr. Creative Mr. Competitive Mr. Complete

*Faith Temple Cathedral Books*

Destiny's Decision  More Than Diamonds

*A Louisiana Love Series*

The Right Choice

The Wrong Decision

The Perfect Chance

*The Blessed Opportunity*

*A Louisiana Christmas*

Love Me Again

Never Looking Back

The Complete Set: A La. Christmas

***The Power Series Rebirth***

Graced After The Pain

Grace Restored

Grace Realized

Grace Revealed

***E Love Series***

Enduring Love

Enchanting Love

Everlasting Love

Extraordinary Love

Extravagant Love

***The Power Series Rebirth***

Graced After The Pain

Grace Restored

Grace Realized

Grace Revealed

The Complete Set: Graced AfterThe Pain

www.ingramcontent.com/pod-product-compliance
Lightning Source LLC
Chambersburg PA
CBHW020929090426
42736CB00010B/1081